The
Secret Sauce
of
Servant Leadership

Seven Ingredients that Ignites the Power of People

Dr. Peter K. Scheuermann

ISBN 979-8-88616-823-5 (paperback)
ISBN 979-8-88616-824-2 (digital)

Christian Faith Publishing
832 Park Avenue
Meadville, PA 16335
www.christianfaithpublishing.com

Printed in the United States of America

CONTENTS

ACKNOWLEDGMENTS

I want to thank my wife Christina, who has been such an encourager and wonderful soul who shows love to everyone despite the circumstance or situation. She sees the good in everyone and has made me a better follower of Christ, filling our home with His love and joy every day.

Second, I want to thank Regent University and the entire staff for their tremendous support and encouragement throughout this doctoral journey. It is so wonderful to see and engage with such great leaders in the workplace who live out their faith and seek the best in others for the Kingdom.

Finally, I want to thank Jesus for walking through this doctoral journey with me, especially when I felt alone or struggled and wanted to give up and drop out of the program. This milestone marks a life goal I have chosen to pursue and use to serve Him wherever He leads me.

INTRODUCTION

Today's leaders often struggle with determining what the right path is for their leadership journey. What education, skill sets, requirements, and contacts should they develop to achieve leadership effectiveness and success? Where do leaders begin to find the right path or guide to achieve leadership success? Servant leadership is an approach everyone can apply both in their work and personal lives. Servant leadership is a leader's complete focus on the follower, for their success and full benefit so much so, the leader will sacrifice their own personal gain and glory. While this approach to leadership is not the only method, everyone can improve by applying a few of its essential characteristics, making themselves more effective and successful in their leadership. This paper addresses these questions by reviewing leadership concepts and topics and identifying the required ingredients needed to develop the secret sauce of servant leadership for today's modern leader to employ. This manuscript was born out of reading and studying several scholarly publications, academic research, and numerous books on organizational development, leadership theories, and practical application content.

Over the last sixty years, servant leadership has emerged as one of the prominent leadership styles for leaders to adopt and employ for organizational success. However, the primary focus of servant leadership is not the success of the organization or the leader, but the follower or individual. Servant leadership focuses on the individual and their ability to grow every day, pursuing self-actualization, and experiencing a life changed for their greater good and all those around them. How is this accomplished given the billions of people who exist on the globe today? Love. Love of people. Love is this primary ingredient and will be discussed later.

This manuscript is designed to help either a new leader just beginning in their leadership journey or someone who has been in leadership roles (people manager or project related) to quickly understand the topics and start employing recommended application actions and behaviors. These chapters in this manuscript are designed to serve as a launching pad to ignite and quickly start a leader down the path of servant leadership. Each chapter is structured with four sections. The first section provides a definition and summary overview of the concept, supported by scholarly research. The second section offers modern-day examples over the last century in individuals and organizations that lived or live out the idea or topic that everyone can relate to. This includes a brief insightful summary of the leader or known organization and the concept or topic they display. The third section is an in-person interview with someone who lives out these characteristics in their profession. Finally, the fourth section is a recommended practical application of the concept that the leader can employ in his or her organization. While this manuscript is written with a strong Christian and biblical perspective including references and examples, the goal is for all readers to gain understanding as to what servant leadership is, and how it can be applied and lived out in everyone's life, no matter spiritual affiliation, position, financial status, or location. The following paragraphs provide a summary each chapter presented in this manuscript.

Chapter 1: What Is Servant Leadership?

This introductory chapter presents and defines the key elements of servant leadership. It provides a review of the origins of servant leadership and introduces the reader to those who have gained global recognition through their research and provided multiple publications to advance the knowledge and application of servant leadership. This chapter is foundational to the seven ingredients of servant leadership, which include the following:

- The Purpose and Calling of a Servant Leader
- The Values of a Servant Leader
- The Vision of a Servant Leader
- The Designing and Building of a High-Performance Culture of Servant Leadership
- The Creation of Trust and Relationships of a Servant Leader
- The Character of a Servant Leader
- Love: The Primary Ingredient of Servant Leadership

These ingredients are presented and discussed in this manuscript with the purpose of introducing the reader to the servant leadership method and providing a detailed analysis of its benefits and challenges.

*Chapter 2: Defining One's Purpose, Calling,
and Vocation as a Servant Leader*

Chapter 2 provides the underpinnings of what it means to find true meaning in a leader's specific vocation and life purpose. A leader's approach to service will define what he or she is called to do and achieve fulfillment for themselves and those they will lead. Much of this chapter will focus on a biblical perspective for leadership.

*Chapter 3: Defining, Determining, and Living
out One's Values as a Servant Leader*

This chapter helps both the leader and the organization determine their values, including both terminal and instrumental values. These two value categories will be defined and discussed in more detail. When values are clearly defined, demonstrated, and lived out through the individuals in the organization, a oneness, and team spirit begin to flourish.

Chapter 4: The Power of a Servant Leaders Vision

Without vision and foresight, a servant leader's organization will remain on the starting line, never taking off down its journey. This chapter helps a leader establish a vision for themself and align their vision with their followers. Through vision, great achievements can be attained; however, this requires a total commitment from everyone.

*Chapter 5: Designing and Building a High-
Performance Culture for Servant Leadership*

Culture is formed by the values and beliefs of an organization. This chapter discusses how a leader can build a culture that can withstand expected change and survived crisis events. Several required elements in this chapter will be discussed for developing and sustaining an organization's culture through the leader and their servant leader characteristics.

Chapter 6: Creating Trust and Long-Lasting Relationships

Trust between two people is formed through a belief in someone who will either agree or follow through on their commitment to another. This chapter dives into what it means to develop and strengthen trust throughout an organization. It includes a discussion on the three forms of trust: contractual, communication, and competence. Leadership trust and the reciprocation from those leaders serve are critical for individual and organizational growth.

Chapter 7: Developing and Sustaining Character as a Servant Leader

Character has always been a difficult concept to understand or develop in a leader's life. Yet all leaders and followers need to continually refine their character to grow and achieve success in their lives. This chapter spends time defining character, what it means to display character, living out its virtues, and most of all, how a leader must continually develop their character.

Chapter 8: Love: The Primary Ingredient for Servant Leadership

This chapter presents the most important ingredient of all for servant leadership—namely, the leader's love for his or her followers in the organization. Without being motivated by the love of people, a leader—no matter their approach or style, will never achieve success. Love is foundational in all relationships in servant leader's life. Servant leadership espouses the love of people as a critical virtue. Here, servant leadership shows up in organizations through love and the continual investment in other's success, so much so that their lives are completely changed for their benefit and the good of others.

One last comment—the reader will note reference to both servant leader and leader throughout the manuscript. These two titles are used interchangeably when a concept or topic is introduced or discussed.

CHAPTER 1

What Is Servant Leadership?

Servant leadership has gained much attention over the last sixty years in academic writing and modern workplace application.[1] Servant leadership is a passion and desire to serve others, namely the follower or least privileged, to give sacrificially without regard for one's personal gain or benefit. While many other leadership theories are practiced in the workplace, such as leader-member exchange, transactional, transformational, and authentic, servant leadership focuses heavily on the follower rather than the leader and his or her success. Servant leaders put a strong emphasis on both personal integrity and service to all people, including fellow employees and people they interact with outside of work in various community organizations.[2] Robert K. Greenleaf, known as the father of the modern-day servant leadership movement,[3] found through his research and writings, that as a leader motivates their followers through positive behavior characteristics, organizations can successfully achieve their goals and profitability at the same time. His research over forty years while employed at AT&T in management research brought forth the idea that both leaders and their organizations can improve the lives of their followers by putting them first in service for their success.

---

[1] (Northhouse 2013).

[2] Liden, Sandy, Zhao, and Henderson, 161.

[3] Greenleaf.

He based his entire premise on the 1965 novel written by Hermann Hesse called *The Journey to the East.* In this novel, a group of travelers went on a journey to the East. Within the group, a servant immerged motivating and inspiring the entire group by his service to them. The servant took on day-to-day chores and tasks to ensure everyone in the group was well taken care of. However, during their travels, the servant became lost, and in his absence, the entire group becomes dismayed, confused, lost, and not sure what direction to take next. This story exemplies a servant was actually the main and most important leader throughout their entire journey. They just did not realize his impact on success of each individual within the group.

According to Greenleaf, "A servant-leader is one who is servant first."[4] Greenleaf goes on to further clarify the servant leader approach in his writing of *The Servant as Leader,*

> It begins with the natural feeling that one wants to serve, to serve first. Then the conscious choice brings one to aspire to lead. The difference manifests itself in the care taken by the servant-first to make sure that other people's highest priority needs are being served. The best test is: Do those served grow as persons; do they, while being served, become healthier, wiser, freer, more autonomous, more likely themselves to become servants?[5]

Over the years, his thoughts, writings, and publications set the standard for further investigation and analysis of what true servant leadership means and how to apply in today's organizations.

While there are multiple servant leadership models,[6] noted servant leadership scholar and author Larry C. Spears studied

---

[4] Spears, 3.
[5] Greenleaf, 13.
[6] (Joseph and Winston 2003).

Greenleaf's writings and categorized the following ten characteristics that embody servant leadership:

1. *Listening.* Servant leaders focus intently on their follower's opinions and perspectives.
2. *Empathy.* Servant leaders desire to understand and have compassion for their followers.
3. *Healing.* Servant leaders seek to help themselves and others to heal emotionally and become whole in well-being while being sensitive to others.
4. *Awareness.* Servant leaders are mindful of their follower's environments and their mindfulness.
5. *Persuasion.* Servant leaders seek to influence followers instead of authority or position.
6. *Conceptualization.* Servant leaders think through complex issues, find creative solutions to problems to achieve the organization's goals.
7. *Foresight.* Servant leaders envision the potential outcome of a situation or dilemma.
8. *Stewardship.* Servant leaders seek to serve the follower first, above all others.
9. *Commitment to the growth of people.* Servant leaders focus on helping the follower grow and succeed, ultimately achieving self-actualization and fullest potential.
10. *Building community.* Servant leaders foster community through shared values and beliefs.[7]

Academic and organizational research suggests that when a leader exemplifies servant leadership characteristics and behaviors to their followers, it results in improved morale, increased trust, higher productivity, and increased revenue growth. The leader and the follower that make up the organization experience increased values alignment with the organizations mission. This drives increased cre-

---

[7] Joseph and Winston, 1.

ativity, innovation, and a complete commitment to service with high employee respect for each other with all people considered equal to each other.[8]

What type of followers would respond well and thrive in a servant leadership environment? Those followers who seek value, significance, equality, purpose, confidence, freedom, and support in a relationship. When leaders develop and grow followers to their fullest potential, organizations achieve success and leader effectiveness. A servant leader seeks to improve all followers in character development, social responsibility, ethical and moral behavior, helping them reach their fullest potential, and ultimately, self-actualization. See Figure 1 for reference.

Figure 1
Servant Leadership Success

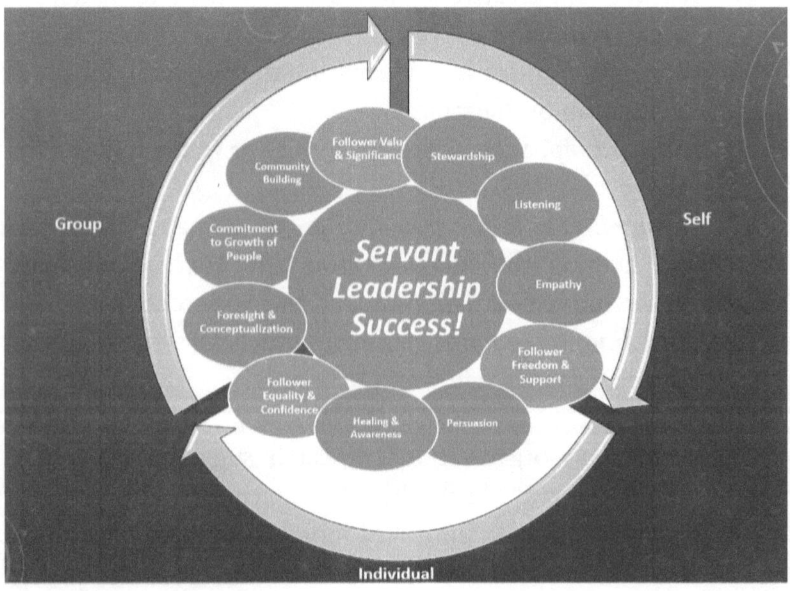

(Adapted from Joseph and Winston 2010, 10; Patterson 2003.)

---

[8] Anderson, 9–10.

While this model, as depicted in Figure 1, serves as the basis for servant leadership characteristics, additional models have emerged over the last twenty years, such as Patterson's model, called the *Model of Constructs of Servant Leadership*[9] offers an alternative view and insight into this modern-day leadership approach. Both of these models will be used as a point of reference throughout this paper. According to Patterson, servant leadership is composed of seven specific characteristics or virtuous constructs:

1. Agapao love. The leader willingly invests and learns the follower's talents and abilities and determines how this can drive their success as an individual. *Agapao* is a greek name for a "moral love," to ethically and morally make the right choices for the right reasons at the apporpriate time.
2. Humility. To acknowledge others above yourself, exalting their accomplishments.
3. Altruism. To be more concerned about the follower's benefit and welfare or good.
4. Vision. The leader sees how a follower's potential can significantly impact society at large.
5. Trust. The leader has complete confidence and belief in the follower to be open and complete tasks as expected.
6. Empowerment. The leader gives responsibility and autonomy to the follower in the assigned tasks or initiatives.
7. Service. The leader putting the follower first above their concerns in meeting their needs beyond all other priorities.[10]

Benefits and Challenges of Servant Leadership

Many modern-day organizations such as Southwest Airlines, Vanguard, Starbucks, and TD Industries have adopted and incorporated servant leadership in their leadership development programs

---

[9] Patterson.
[10] Patterson, 3–6.

to put the follower first, in puruit for their success and well-being. While servant leadership focuses mainly on the follower and their success, recent research has shown this approach to have several significant positive organizational outcomes. For instance, both leaders and followers are inspired to achieve increased moral and motivation to serve others.[11] Modern-day organizations must consider how they can remain focused on developing adaptable or agile environments yet keep the follower focused for their growth and development as individuals, transforming them into servant leaders.

However, this modern-day leadership approach also has several challenges, such as inconsistent behaviors and experiences, followers not aligning to the vision, dissimilar goals, short-term productivity loss, and individual irregular behavioral responses to servant leadership. While most organizations espouse common ideals, groups/divisions are quite the opposite in pursuit of individual personal goals instead of the big picture of the success of everyone as a whole. Second, servant leadership enables followers to take responsibility, empowering them to complete tasks without oversight by the leader. Is the leader and the organization willing to take this risk with their followers in their attempts to integrate servant leadership characteristics and behaviors into their organizations? Growth can only happen through new experiences and taking risks. Is the organization willing to accept short-term profitability loss? Third, not every employee will respond positively to servant leadership. Some leaders base their entire leadership style and approach on very basic, fundamental transactional relationships, such as sales-focused roles where employees react to a financial reward as the only form of motivation, vs. servant leadership with positive feedback, individual consideration, and career growth. Figure 2 provides additional benefits and challenges to servant leadership.

---

[11] Burns, 20.

Figure 2
Benefits and Challenges

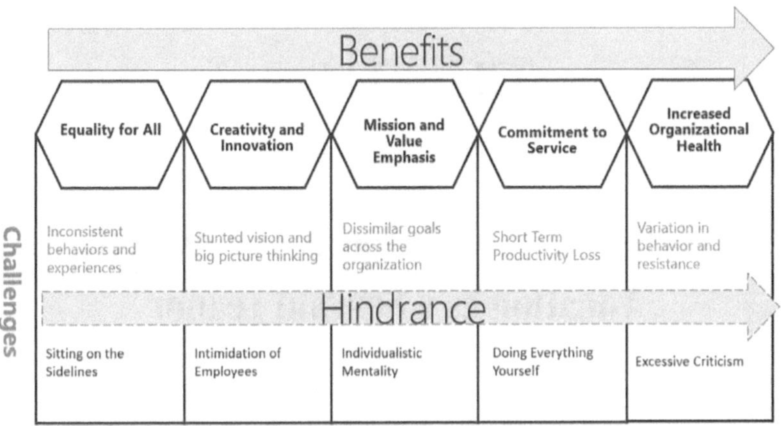

(Anderson 2009, 9–11)

This *Model of Constructs* from Patterson demonstrates how each of these virtues works in tandem, beginning with Agapeo Love and finish with Service. All examples used in this manuscript have several elements in common. They all emphasize service to the individual as a primary focus, they expressed influence on society for good, and they all experienced success because of thier servant leadership approach. Throughout this manuscript, both models will be used as reference artifacts for theory and practical application.

CHAPTER 2

Defining One's Purpose, Calling, and Vocation as a Servant Leader

Leaders and followers of all ages often ask, what is my purpose? What is my calling here? What vocation should I pursue? What is my God-given talent/s, and how should I use them? How do I achieve fulfillment in this life? Many people spend most of their lives asking these questions and never come to the realization of these answers. The following section will provide insights, modern-day examples, and practical application for servant leaders to catapult the understanding of their purpose, calling, and future vocation in service.

The concept of someone's purpose is often asked through a common question of "why do I exist?"[12] and what is expected of me, especially in my current circumstance? How do I know I am doing the right thing? These questions are not easily answered when taking a broad or surface level approach without deep thought and reasoning. However, when individuals discern their purpose, they often become focused to fulfilling their purpose, exuberating confidence, and joy, knowing their path in life. So how is this question answered? While there will be more details and steps to follow in the practical

---

[12] Deterding, 6.

application section, determining one's purpose will likely come from answering the question, "Why do I get out of bed and begin my day?" What about those who willfully sacrifice their time and lives going above and beyond for the rest of society, such as police officers, firefighters, first responders, doctors, who continually face dire circumstances that may require them to give up their lives for society's safety and good.

While there are cases where some individuals find this is not their calling and passion, the general population of people in these occupations are considered servant leaders and know this is what they were called to do. In the face of fatalities, what makes them get up the next day and continue in their work, knowing this is the purpose of what God has intended for them. Do they find joy and fulfillment? It is the author's opinion that only the person who accepts what God has designed for their purpose will answer yes to this question. When a servant leader realizes their purpose, all other decisions and choices are far easier to make. In addition, a leader's passion and desire to serve those around them will become magnified all the more, driving growth and achievement of self-actualization.[13] Life purposes can be categorized into three areas, personal, family, and professional. Individual purpose could bes to serve as a follower of Christ in all interactions from the beginning of the day till the end. Family purpose would encompass to be the best father/mother, grandfather/grandmother, husband/wife, and good neighbor to the local community. Professional purpose could be to help others achieve character development, fulfillment in their lives, increasing skills and knowledge for excellence in service, and evangelize servant leadership to all. Again, the practical application section will help define a leader's purpose in addition to calling and vocation, which will be discussed next.

Determining a calling takes purpose to greater depths of understanding and meaning. First, to define calling, according to Greenleaf, calling is a purposeful, divinely inspired thought process

---

[13] D'Souza and Gurin.

and behavioral act to serve others. However, Dik and Duffy further clarify calling stating:

> A calling is a transcendent summons, experienced as originating beyond the self, to approach a particular life role in a manner oriented toward demonstrating or deriving a sense of purpose or meaningfulness and that holds other-oriented values and goals as primary sources of motivations.[14]

Here, servant leaders see and feel a divine intervention from God, the supernatural coming down to the natural, imposing a desire or passion toward a particular goal or objective to accomplish. Some may view this desire manifest itself in the natural from relations and experiences with other people. The draw and passion lead the servant leader to find peace in the calling and, ultimately, fulfillment in their lives, thereby contributing to the greater good of society. This definition leads the servant leader to understand role definition is not required; just sacrificial service to others achieves the goal of a calling on a leader or follower's life. No matter the role or work, every Christians have a calling to serve God in whatever capacity or environment. However, is it a requirement to be a Christian to be a servant leader? No, servant leadership, while has many ties and aligment to Christianity, it is also found in several other religions and beliefs across the globe such as Judaism, Hinduism, and Toa religions.

Through the servant leader's selfless and sacrificial acts, they will gain respect and confidence from their followers, often requiring many acts and over significant a defined time period. Christians believe that every human being is called by God to a specific role or activity to serve. Christ said that to be great in His Kingdom, His followers must learn to be servants of all. Christians are called to

---

[14] Dik and Duffy, 427.

serve no matter the task, situation, environment, circumstance, or situation.

Historically, the term "calling" has been understood as God bestowing specific talents and abilities on each individual for a particular task or role to serve. Although, recent scholarly research has secularized the concept of calling to mean "finding personal fulfillment in one's work and perceiving work as meaningful and purposeful."[15] Calling comes from the heart, the heart in God in all of His believers with a passion and urgency to change the world, to continually love God and love one's neighbor, building the kingdom of God.

Christians are servant leaders serving in Christ's Kingdom as His children, whom he calls friends[16] who are heirs to His Kingdom. So how does a leader determine their calling for service? While this question has been asked by countless people over the years and will continue to be asked, there is a straightforward answer: *service to others and God.* Calling gives meaning to a leader's life, especially when a leader invests for the greater good of others, without recognition or reward. Barbuto and Wheeler posit, "Calling is fundamental to servant leadership and have operationalized it as a desire to serve and willingness to sacrifice self-interest for the benefit of others."[17] When individuals consciously decide to serve others through sacrificial giving, God works in their lives and ignites the fruit of the spirit: love, joy, peace, patience, kindness, goodness, faithfulness, and self-control.[18] How does a servant leader find themselves? Begin with first identifying with Christ. Philippians 2:22 states, "Work out your salvation with fear and trembling, for it is God who works in you to will and to do of his good pleasure" (NIV). The Christian belongs to the body of Christ, and it is through this identity, their calling becomes evident over time.

A Christian often asks, what type of work is God calling them to do, and whom do they do it with? The occupation they choose

---

[15] Steger et al., 83.
[16] Agosto.
[17] Barbuto and Wheeler, 304–305.
[18] Gal. 5:22–23.

and those they serve will likely change several times throughout their life. God does call His people to perform specific work and projects. For example, Nehemiah, a servant to King Artaxerxes who served as a cupbearer,[19] was called to rebuild the temple wall in Jerusalem.[20] Joseph, a servant in Potiphar's house, was called to lead his entire household servants,[21] serving in whatever capacity God gave him. Both of their callings were not necessarily a specific vocation for the rest of their lives, but more so a calling to service, no matter the work or activity. However, God does lead His people to specific occupations and roles throughout their lives. In biblical terms, calling is a much deeper concept with Christ, directing His followers as to His plan and His purpose for his or her entire life including professional and personal pursuits. A calling in a servant leader in Christ's Kingdom penetrates the individual's heart, changing and molding their state of being for greatness in his Kingdom. When a leader or follower accepts the call to follow Christ, His spirit becomes active within the leader and in every aspect of their life. However, a calling to follow Christ does not automatically mean a call into a professional church position or ministerial occupation. While some are called to do just that, all Christians, no matter occupation or role, are equally called to live a spirit-filled life of service, modeling the way for all to see and experience.[22]

So how does a servant leader become attuned to God's calling in their life? While the practical application section will give specific guidance, the following steps can be employed at a high level. First, practice active listening[23] through daily prayer, reading, and mediating on scripture. Second, begin to serve others within various organizations such as schools, churches, and other community-related organizations for impact. Third, seek mentors or wise counsel.

---

[19] Crowther.

[20] Neh. 1–2.

[21] Gen. 39.

[22] Kouzes and Posner.

[23] Barbuto and Wheeler, 10.

Leading international scholar and author Michael Novak provides four characteristics or "Power Points"[24] of a calling on one's life:

1. *The calling is unique to each person.* The leader or follower has a deep passion and desire to engage in a particular type of work that only a subset group of other people have the same desire. Not everyone is designed or equipped to be lawyers, doctors, policemen, or airline pilots, to name a few.

2. *The calling has specific requirements for success.* First, the leader must have the talent, including the mental and physical capabilities, to fulfill the role. Essentially, does one have the commitment and passion for continuing in the journey when the struggle becomes natural, and you are alone in your pursuit of the calling? Will and can you withstand the resistance and potentially overbearing burdens while living out your calling?

3. *Joy and peace in the struggle.* Will you still find joy and happiness, even in the face of difficulty and setbacks? People who deal with fatalities every day may not be pleasant, know their calling and purpose is to serve in those roles.

4. *Facing setbacks, roadblocks, and failure to find your calling.* Through many trials and errors over time, only a calling to a particular work or assignment is made apparent. Be prepared to experience "false starts" and "do-overs" to discover where God may be calling you to serve.[25]

The Impact of Calling on Vocation

A leader and follower's vocation is often the type of work or career they have chosen or current position to serve. This, quite often, is not associated with a particular religious organization or institu-

---

[24] Spears, 34.

[25] Novak.

tion. According to Dik and Duffy, "A vocation is an approach to a particular life role that is oriented toward demonstrating or deriving a sense of purpose or meaningfulness and that holds other-oriented values and goals as primary sources of motivation."[26]

While there is a coinciding or blending of a calling and a vocation, there is clear distinction between the two. However, when individuals connect their vocation, their daily work, and their calling to serve others, there is a supernatural phenomenon in their lives. They find deep fulfillment in purpose and meaning in their lives, knowing this is God's will and His ultimate purpose being fulfilled! So what should a servant leader do to ensure they are in the right vocation, even if this is not what they desire or feel they should be doing? Accept the current situation or circumstance, even if it is less than desirable. Then ask, what can be learned or achieved from this experience? How can a leader make a difference and improve the current environment and the people they serve? A leader should keep their focus on Kingdom service through behavioral acts of excellence toward those they engage with.

Examples of Purpose and Calling in Modern-Day Organizations and Servant Leaders

Purpose and calling are crucial to servant leaders and their followers. Leaders from both the Old and New Testament were motivated by a sense of calling and purpose to obey, honor, and please their master. The following narrative will provide biblical and modern-day examples of organizations and individual leaders who embraced these concepts and changed the world. While their circumstances and situations may be unique, they all sought God for direction and employed servant leadership characteristics to accomplish their mission through their purpose of service and obedience to their calling.

---

[26] Dik and Duffy, 428.

Nehemiah (cupbearer, superintendent to rebuilding the wall)

The book of Nehemiah, written 445–432 BC,[27] records Israel's third return to Jerusalem after their captivity, detailing how the walls and the Israelites' broken lives were rebuilt, becoming a great nation again. Nehemiah, a Jewish exile as a cupbearer slave to King Artaxerxes, employed continual prayer to receive his calling from God to rebuild Jerusalem's temple walls. While Nehemiah did in fact accept the calling to lead the physical effort in rebuilding the temple walls, his first calling was to help heal and rebuild the broken lives of the Israelite people. His excellence in service to the king granted him permission to fulfill his mission and vision, remaining obedient to God's call on his life. Nehemiah purposely took the time to pray, seeking God's direction as a humble servant, comparing himself to Moses as God's servant.[28] This request and the permission to go, especially to a Jew, rarely if ever happened; however, God's hand and favor were upon Nehemiah's life and mission.[29]

Nehemiah led the Israelites in rebuilding the temple wall in Jerusalem, but more importantly, he helped heal and rebuild the lives of God's people through his servant leadership approach.[30] Jerusalem was the capital and a holy city, representing national identity and God's continual blessings upon Israel. While Nehemiah had never been to his ancestorial homeland, he had a deep passion and love to return in service to rebuild the wall for the Israelite people, reuniting, healing, and bonding them, removing the shame as a conquered and broken-spirited people.[31] This was the third attempt and significant last step to rebuild the temple and, most importantly, rebuild the lives of God's broken and fragmented people.[32] While Nehemiah had position, power, status, and excellent organization skills, he always

---

27 Britannica.

28 Crowther, 59.

29 Neh. 2:3–4 (NIV).

30 Crowther.

31 Maclariello.

32 Neh. 1:3 (NIV).

showed humility, knowing nothing could be accomplished without God's empowerment and strength. He was not a carpenter or builder by profession, yet he knew God would inspire and direct at the right time. In Judah, he arrived with opposition from Sanballat the Horonite, governor of Samaria, and Tobiah, the Ammonite, governor of Transjordan, who came from "neighboring towns."[33] However, despite strong opposition, he continued in his mission, knowing his purpose and calling from God through prayer, fasting, and devotion to God.

Nehemiah was committed in his purpose and service to his leadership position, but more importantly, to God in faithful devotion and trust,[34] accomplishing everything with excellence. Nehemiah saught God through continual prayer, and as a result, God blessed his work. Nehemiah was previously a cupbearer to King Artaxerxes and chose to leave this role for the mission and vision God had placed upon him. This passion caused Nehemiah to abandon his current life of service to his earthly master and transform in service to God, his spiritual master.

Nehemiah had no prior governing, training, or building skills for the rebuilding of the temple wall. However, God bestowed upon him the needed servant leadership characteristics of love, humility, altruism, vision, trust, empowerment, and service[35] to achieve success in his calling to fulfill God's plan as a servant leader.

Joseph (servant to Potiphar, lead prisoner in jail)

The book of Genesis, written 1450–1410 BC, the is first book of the Pentateuch[36] and means beginning. The purpose of Genesis was to record the creation of the universe and God's people, the Israelites, and his desire to have them set apart for exclusive worship to

---

[33] Maclariello, 403.

[34] Hertzburg.

[35] Winston, August 2003.

[36] Sweeney, 15.

Him. It is believed that Moses, a servant leader,[37] authored the entire Pentateuch, composed of four additional books: Exodus, Leviticus, Numbers, and Deuteronomy.[38] However, the author would also like to add that Genesis is known as book of hope and encouragement. No matter how dark and evil the world may seem, God is in total control with a plan and a purpose.

Like Moses, Joseph is also considered one of the greatest heroes in the bible as recorded in Genesis 37:1 to 50:26 (NIV). He served in several servant leader roles such as shepherd, household slave, prison convict and then administrator, and finally, as prime minister of Egypt. Joseph often found himself in multiple dire, life-threatening and circumstances, yet he kept his faith and hope in God for a better tomorrow; no matter the situation, God would guide and direct. However, his life was exemplified with personal integrity, spiritual sensitivity, and led with purpose in all he did.

Genesis 39:1–23 (NIV) demonstrates Joseph's galvanized love, trust, patience, and peace with God, which pulled him through in every hopeless and catastrophic situation, knowing his purpose and calling, no matter the circumstance. Joseph was a slave known for his consistency in excellence of service to all he engaged. While he served his earthly master Potiphar, he also maintained a close and devoted relationship with God in prayer and worship. Joseph stayed faithful to his spiritual connection, sensitive to His calling of service.[39] He always brought forth total commitment in service to God, his ultimate master, above his earthly master. The call on his life was evident. Everything he did was blessed and noticed by those in leadership, including Potiphar, who placed him in charge of his entire household. The prison warden put him in charge of the other prisoners after being thrown into prison. All leaders need a moral compass such as God to keep them centered and at peace, especially during a crisis. This is one of the advantages of being a biblical servant leader.

---

[37] Ben–Hur and Jonsen, 968.
[38] Sweeney, 15.
[39] Patterson.

Second, Joseph was a man who practiced both humility and humble submission as a servant leader. While he displayed several of servant leadership's key characteristics throughout Genesis chapters 37 to 50 of love, service, trust, vision, altruism, and empowerment, humility was a core focus of his leadership in this passage. Joseph rose quickly from slave to second in command within the Egyptian ruling power for Potiphar's household and the prison. He knew this was God's plan and kept his "accomplishments and talents in perspective…not being self-focused but rather focused on others."[40] Joseph modeled the way of servant leadership for others to embrace and lead. According to academic author and scholar Skip Bell, "Those who submit also lead."[41] He knew that becoming great in God's Kingdom was through a servant's heart in the obedience of submission to his spiritual master first, above all else. This pericope demonstrates that even someone who is an outsider to the ruling group or class can earn respect and recognition for their talents and abilities.

Third, Joseph's authenticity and character elevated him to a position of power quickly, extending, building, and challenging servant leadership's virtues. Joseph had full authority and capacity to use all of Potiphar's household assets and resources as he desired. His integrity and character as a faithful servant shined brightly when he repeatedly refused to engage in sexual relations with Potiphar's wife.

Joseph fully understood his role and authority with its limitations and boundaries. He showed his commitment to faithfully serve Potiphar and honor his earthly and spiritual master, running from sinful pleasures and wrongdoing. His deep conviction of complete moral and ethical behavior at all times demonstrated his authentic leadership.[42] Authenticity in leaders requires a continual examination of those servant leader virtues highlighted earlier, ensuring they are in check and continual development.

---

[40] Patterson, 3.
[41] Bell, 222.
[42] Northouse, 254.

Manny Ohonme (Samaritan's Feet, CEO)

The title of Manny's latest book, *Sole Purpose: Shoes of Hope From the Feet of a Samaritan* (Ohonme 2009).

Emmanuel "Manny" Ohonme, serves as Chief Operating Officer (CEO) of Samaritan's Feet International, which touches the lives of children across the globe through shoe distribution. Manny discovered his purpose and calling in life as a young boy in Lagos, Nigeria, to encourage and inspire hope through a pair of shoes. His life transformation began when he received his first pair of shoes at the age of nine leading up to his arrival in America alone through a college basketball scholarship. This event catapulted his purpose and calling as a servant leader, providing shoes to those in need and bringing forth hope for tomorrow and a better future for all.

Manny's story begins with him in the early 1970s as a young boy in Lagos, Nigeria, where a Christian missionary from Wisconsin offered to participate in a competition to win a free pair of shoes. To Manny, the opportunity to just have a chance to win or earn a free pair of shoes was a dream come true. Manny would win the contest and inspire his purpose and calling later in life to create and lead Samaritan's Feet International. (SFI). In Manny's book *Sole Purpose* he states that these sports-ministry missionaries were

> doing something similar to what Samaritan's Feet does today, acting as ambassadors for Christ in poor communities around the world. They came to play with us and run sports camps, to give us a few hours to help us forget our impoverished state. They opened up a world of love, compassion, and grace.[43]

Manny did not start with SFI initially after college. Manny, like Nehemiah, held various secular executive roles in his early years,

---

[43] Ohonme, 32–33.

ascending across multiple leadership roles in the technology industry through the early 2000s. However, during a trip to his hometown in early 2003, his true purpose, God's calling on his life of service to others through the birthing of SFI became evident. Manny's focus became crystal clear in making a difference to those from his hometown and millions of people across the globe, distributing shoes, improving quality of life, and inspiring hope. His purpose and calling truly embody servant leadership by first taking care of the physical needs in providing shoes for improving health and educational opportunities to travel and grow. However, Manny and SFI's purpose extends beyond just the individual physical needs, as they impact thousands across the globe with encouragement and hope to achieve more in their lives than just what is presently seen and experienced.

Southwest Airlines

Purpose: Connect people to what's important in their lives through friendly, reliable, and low-cost air travel.

Southwest Airlines

Southwest Airlines Co. (NYSE: LUV) is a leader in commercial aviation, is known for setting records and continually achieving profits year over year. In 2008, its income was $178 million, including over 100 million customers and employees exceeding 35,000.[44] Compared to 2019, their net income was $2.3 billion, with over 134.1 million customers and more than 60,000 workers. Deterding posits, "Southwest Airlines is an airline phenomenon."[45] In 1967, founder and CEO Herb Kelleher and co-founder Rollin King began Southwest Airlines, with service to three specific city locations: Dallas, Houston, and San Antonio. Today, SWA is now a major carrier across several major US cities and has expanded its destinations

---

[44] (Dierendonck and Patterson 2010).
[45] Deterding, 7.

outside the continental US to Hawaii, Cozumel, and Mexico. What does this all have to do with its purpose as an organization and servant leadership? It has everything to do with it.

When the leader and their organization know their purpose, they can make decisions and act more confidently for the organization's good. SWA's purpose since its inception over forty years ago is "connect people to what's important in their lives through friendly, reliable, and low-cost air travel" (www.southwest.com). Purpose and profitability have a direct correlation here. For SWA to achieve recognition with customers, especially those who could not afford to pay high for the high costs of an airline ticket, they had to keep operating costs down. The focus of everyone at SWA is delivering excellent customer service to its customers, treating them with respect and fairness in maintaining the costs to the customer low, compared to all other airline carriers whose rates are much higher. Because SWA knows its purpose, they can make quick decisions to ensure costs stay low and continue to attract new and returning customers. Each employee evaluates and makes decisions based upon the advancement of SWA's purpose as a business. Having an exciting purpose also drives passion where employees look forward to coming to work and take pride in being part of a great organization. At SWA, the focus is on serving the customer and each other in the organization, so everyone wins. Because they all focus on keeping the fares low, the skies became democratized for everyone to participate (Kelleher and King's vision for SWA). Here servant leadership is at its best because all employees, from the CEO to the pilots, stewards, baggage handlers, and mechanics, all focus on service to one another, ingrained in their culture, values, and beliefs. CEO Kelleher modeled servant leadership across the organization, ensuring it fully reached and impacted every employee. SWA's purpose through low operating costs and excellence in service to all drives and will continue to drive the success at SWA.

Insights on Examples

Determining a purpose for both the leader and follower is not something that is often discovered right away. In most cases, it takes years of experience, trial and error, and just time for purpose to become apparent, as these examples have shown. Several insights are brought forth from these modern-day examples. First, obedience is one of the hardest things for anyone or organization, for that matter, to willfully submit to. Both Joseph and Nehemiah faced unexpected and insurmountable conflicts, resistance, and struggles in carrying out their purpose. Manny Ohonme took a significant risk in giving up his career and financial comforts to start a nonprofit shoe ministry from nothing because he felt God's purpose and calling on his life. Most would ignore and continue in the life they have created for themselves. Southwest Airlines took a radically different approach to become a profitable business with low airfares. Given this approach, they will have to remain vigilant and innovative in maintaining their low fare cost while employing excellence in service to all methodology.

What is vital for the servant leader and the follower is to understand everyone has a purpose and mission on this earth, and that is to serve others with one's unique talents and abilities, sharing one's resources. Past accomplishments should be predicated on what has been done for others and how they impacted their lives for their good and thier future. When a person serves others with passion and dedication, he or she achieves fulfillment in purpose, and our calling becomes a life of service to all. Every human being has a gift to share with others that can change the world for the good of others. Christians, are to love God and let His purpose become alive and vibrant in their lives as he or she lives out a life of servitude through the calling of service. The most significant accomplishment for a leader in achieving fulfillment in purpose is their legacy through the positive influence on their followers.

An interview with Dr. Timothy Cheuvront, owner of
Cheuvront Clinic of Chiropractic and Sports Medicine

Dr. Cheuvront has been improving the quality of patient's lives for more than thirty years. Upon graduating from the prestigious National University of Health Sciences in 1989, Dr. Cheuvront opened his first chiropractic practice in Canandaigua, New York, until 1996. He then moved his family to the Charlotte, North Carolina, region and opened the Cheuvront Clinic of Chiropractic and Sports Medicine in the beautiful town of Matthews, North Carolina. Dr. Cheuvront and his wife Lori have three grown children, Joshua, Rachel and Ryan, and two grandchildren, Bridget and Caroline. Dr. Cheuvront has been a member of the Matthews Chamber of Commerce for over twenty years and served as a board member from 2012 to 2016 and in 2014, Chamber president. Over the last twenty-five years, Dr. Cheuvront has continually served as a board member and elected officer positions of several community nonprofit organizations such as the Kiwanis Club, chairman of Deacons at Hickory Grove Baptist Church, former president of the Hickory Grove Christian School's booster club and school board, and the Matthews HELP Center from 2012 to 2015. Dr. Cheuvront currently leads the North Carolina Chiropractic Association for the Central South District.

How did you discover your purpose or calling? While a sophomore in college, I was hit from behind of my body three times in separate car accidents. The typical treatment I was provided was muscle relaxers and other mediations. These medications caused issues with studies, and I finally chose a chiropractor to treat my problems. I truly found this profession fascinating and chose this as my career. I also liked the career aspect of a chiropractor vs. a medical doctor. I truly wanted a family life and this fit my desires of a lifestyle I wanted to live. The calling on my life was from a healing perspective. I really didn't get the calling until I realized I was changing the body in a way to heal itself. It is unbelievable that I am part of this to re-align the person's spin or abnormally they have. I am still amazed at how this all works. You don't realize how good something is till you are involved more deeply.

What were the signs in your life that helped you discover your purpose as a servant leader? When I was growing up as a young boy, I had several family members living close, taking care of my brothers, sisters, and cousins—always organizing and leading the football, kickball, and baseball games. I always looked out for the team I was on.

As I progressed into high school, I would organize fundraisers and enjoyed leading. It started early and continued to evolve. I am not the greatest as a follower, but I often see things that can be improved and automatically lead. This is something you practice over time and develop. People realize you like to do these leadership roles and then are asked to take on board-related positions.

What shaped your thoughts and path, forming your purpose and mission in life? My Christian faith formed this. When the Apostle Paul left on his last mission, he specifically said to take care of the widows and orphans; I felt my desire to serve in this area. I am reminded of Luke 12:48, "From everyone who has been given much, much will be demanded; and from the one who has been entrusted with much, much more will be asked." Whatever I can do in the community to help other organizations, I want to contribute to help grow and nurture. The deacons took care of the feeding and cooking for the orphans and widows.

Tell me something unique or significant along your life's path as a servant leader. Being involved in various organizations, I am somewhat disheartened by those involved from a checklist perspective. Some get on boards for personal gain or acknowledgment, not because of their passion for the organization and how their contributions will change lives for the better. I try to see the best in people, and when I don't see this, it is disappointing.

I always know when I am called to serve because I am all in with a passion to serve. When it turns into work, I lose the feeling of the calling. Someone else needs to step in and lead. Sometimes you could be a roadblock to another person who may be the next leader to lead that organization. I usually serve two to three times in an organization and then step down. I feel the spirit moving in me to lead or when it is time to gracefully exit.

Where do you think individuals and organizations fail in discovering or misunderstand their purpose and calling?

For individuals, when my wife and I were reading books to our kids at an early age, we read to our children as if we were putting a paintbrush in their hand, not a scalpel. We put a paintbrush in their hand to give God the glory. The easy thing is to say about one's calling is to go where the money is. That is not the right path. My wife was the most perfect path in math during her academic years. Her guidance counselor suggested computer science, and she wanted to teach young children. She chose to teach and loves her job! I don't know anyone else who loves her teaching career more than my wife.

New leaders often try to make their mark early on in their organization. Or change for the sake of making change. For example, I was on a local nonprofit board, and they fired the executive director when in reality, the organization just needed tweaking, not complete removal of its leader. This is where mistakes begin to immerge. If the desire is to change the organization and your change does not align with the mission statement, you need to back away from this.

What would you recommend to individuals and organizations trying to define or redefine their purpose or calling? Your mission or statement has to be short, sweet, and specific. If too encompassing, vague, or all-encompassing, you will lose motivation, and people who follow you will too. If you know the direction you are going in, that creates passion.

Practical Application: Determining Your Purpose, Calling, and Vocation (PCV)

So how should a leader and a follower discern their purpose, calling, and vocation? Is there a surefire method or approach that delivers the answer to these sought-after questions? As discussed before, sometimes people spend most of their lives trying to answer these questions, but often approach them the wrong way. Every person is given a unique set of talents and abilities for their calling and purpose through a vocation. The key is to discern early on and take action towards those objectives. The following recommended actions or steps (they don't have to be in the same order) will help every individual with their purpose, calling, and vocation. These steps perfectly align with several of the servant leadership characteristics discussed earlier in this manuscript. See Figure 2.1 below.

Listening

Spears recommends listening as a first step in determining your purpose and calling. Greenleaf's earlier writing supports this by stating, "a true; natural servant automatically responds to a problem by listening first."[46] Active listening requires a conscious, purposeful commitment to understand and communicate effectively with others. Seek what others or groups are trying to communicate and validate your understanding before taking action. Often, a leader will experience an "inner voice,"[47] directing them as to where their heart is. Does the leader have a feeling or passion around what they are hearing? Active listening is a core characteristic of a servant leader. While active listening requires effort and focus, so does spending time alone in reflection. Many organizations hold leadership retreats away from their main offices for their executive leadership to focus on listening to each other and evaluating and strategizing their plans, employing strategic foresight.[48] Leaders should note their surroundings and couple this with what has been communicated by their followers before making any significant plans or critical decisions.

Prayer, God's Word, and Wise Counsel

Prayer and daily reading of God's Word is so essential in the grounding of a Christian servant leader. Through prayer and reflection, a leader find thier inner calm and state of peace. God will reveal his plan through a committed daily scripture reading and study, much as he did with Nehemiah, Joseph, Manny Ohonme, and Herb Kelleher. Trust that God will provide the right words and talents at the right time as he speaks through that still inner voice. Also, seek counsel and wise mentors who can help discern your future. For example, I usually have lunch with peers five and ten years older than me to gain their insights into what they see as future opportu-

---

[46] Greenleaf, 7.

[47] Spears, 4.

[48] (Hines 2006).

nities to grow and develop. I often ask the question, "If you were in my shoes at my current age, what would have you done differently if anything?" This question will either validate the right path in a leader's purpose or adjust the coordinates to a leader's future vocation. Think of other servant leaders who will give honest, candid, and constructive feedback to grow and strengthen character What modeling attributes can be gained from those who are wise counsel? What leadership traits can be developed from those interactions?

Record and Document Your Journey: Developing a PCV Journal

Leaders should keep a journal of your daily or weekly experiences so they can look back and see how God has lead and developed them along the journey. A leader must be open and honest with thier feelings (good and bad), so they see how, through their struggle, they have grown and overcome situations and circumstances in their pursuit of purpose, calling, and vocation (PCV). A leader should create and build a PCV plan highlighting their strengths, weaknesses, and those areas that bring joy and fulfillment. A leader should tune into those areas of pleasure and fulfillment to refine the scope of thier purpose and calling. They should actively pray and ask God for his intervention and guidance in this plan.

Once a leader's PCV is defined, they should determine those areas that bring peace, execute the PCV plan, and continually reflect and revise as needed. How long will this take? When will a leader know they have finally found purpose, calling, and vocation? Only when they can say, "I am receiving fulfillment in my life and want to serve others to experience this same feeling in the same manner."

Service to others

Service to others helps individuals take their minds off their current circumstances and focuses on helping others. When a leader struggles within themself, not knowing what brings joy and fulfillment in their lives, they should consider volunteering at a soup kitchen, a homeless shelter, a nonprofit ministry, or an organization in their community. For a leader to find themself, they need to lose their life in service to others. Service will ultimately lead to thier purpose, calling, and eventual vocation.

Remain Curious and Open to New Ideas

Leaders should always be vigilant and open to new ideas from others. Often, the answer or solution is right in front of them. A leader should be open to innovation and new approaches to determine their next steps as a servant leader and thier organization to determine their purpose and calling. The people a leader daily engages with, usually has the answers they are seeking.

Figure 2.1
An iterative process to achieving and maintaining
servant leader purpose, calling, and vocation.

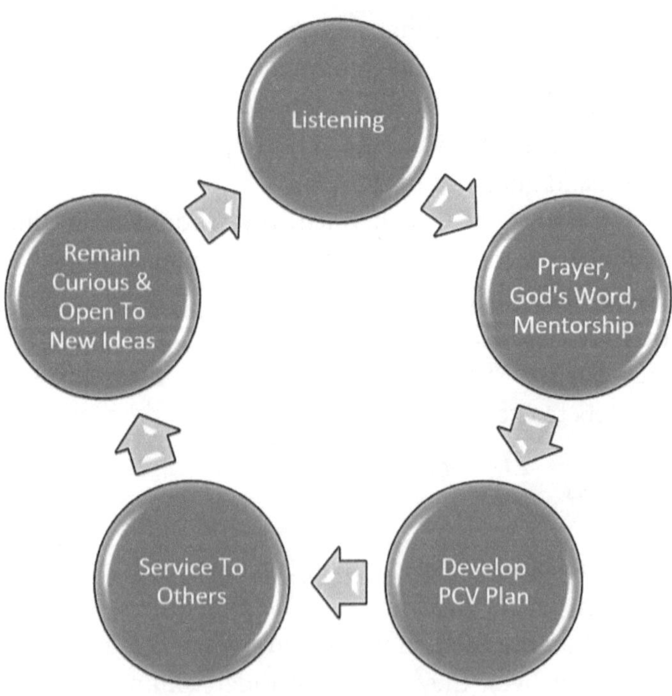

CHAPTER 3

Defining, Determining, and Living out One's Values

All organizations have their own unique culture and values that they align and live by. Culture, defined by Schein is "a pattern of shared basic assumptions learned by a group as it solved its problems of external adaptation and internal integration."[49] What does this mean regarding servant leadership,[50] and how should a leader employ these characteristics in leading today's organizations? This chapter will provide insights into what culture and values are, modern-day examples in leaders and organizations, and practical application for servant leaders to build and sustain values within themselves and the organization they serve.

Individual and organizational values are directly related to human needs. Human beings, as compared to animals, have free will in how to respond to others. All people base thier responses and choices on the beliefs they are willing to fight or even die for. "A primary function of values is to meet needs."[51] Abraham Maslow, psychologist and philosopher, known for his work on the self-actualization theory, posits the basic needs of all humans of social, safety, and

---

[49] Schein, 18.
[50] (Spears 1998)
[51] Gellerman and Hultman, 3.

physiological must be met first before ultimately achieving esteem and self-actualization.

Values and needs are directly related. Rokeach posits values, value systems and needs:

> A *value* is an enduring belief that a specific mode of conduct or end-state of existing is personally or socially preferable to an opposite or converse mode of conduct or end-state of existence. A value system is an enduring organization of beliefs concerning preferable modes of conduct or end-states of existing along a continuum of relative importance.[52]

A servant leader should seek to help followers move up the hierarchy beyond those basic needs to reach self-actualization and then further motivate those followers to help others achieve self-actualization or state of being. How do values relate to organizational culture?

Organizational culture is composed of individual and corporate values. These can overlap or be utterly distinct from each other. A servant leader must be sensitive and attuned to these values and work to build a harmonious organization based upon them. Cameron and Quinn state, "The concept of culture refers to the taken-for-granted values, underlying assumptions, expectations, and definitions that characterize organizations and their members."[53] Culture can also be thought of as the "social glue binding an organization together."[54] In plain terms, culture is how people identify themselves with the organization, make decisions, behave, accomplish their work, and set expectations on how they will socially interact. These form the basis of the values of each contributor to the organization. Terminal and instrumental values make up an organizations' culture.

---

[52] Rokeach, 5.
[53] Cameron and Quinn, 8.
[54] Cameron and Quinn, 18.

Terminal values are goals a leader would like to achieve or continually pursue throughout their lifetime. They are often an ideal instead of an absolute, such as equality for all, a world at peace, self-respect, national security, and freedom. While these pursuits may never come to full fruition, people still pursue them as their inner core desires to contribute and make a difference in these areas for themselves and the good of all others. These values are considered end-states of existence.[55] "Terminal values are fundamental to an organization's mission and vision. A team's mission and vision might differ somewhat from those of the overall organization but, to avoid potential conflict, there must be enough alignment for progress toward the overall mission and vision to be achieved."[56]

Table 1
Terminal Value Examples

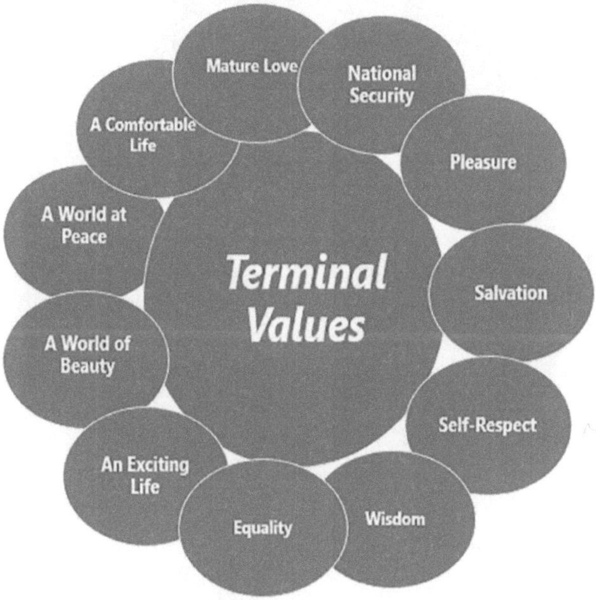

---

[55] (Gellerman and Hultman 2002).
[56] Rokeach, 80.

Instrumental values are often called "preferred modes of conduct,"[57] to accomplish or achieve the terminal value realization. Being sincere, honest, ambitious, and ethical behavior are a few examples. These values focus on the behavior and actions of both the leader and the followers in the organization. Instrumental values also work closely together, driving the organization's culture and become the resistance to change. A leader's character often shines through instrumental values.

Table 2
Instrumental Value Examples

---

[57] Gellerman and Hultman, 5.

Examples of Values in the Workplace

The following narrative will provide several examples of individual and organizational values in modern-day organizations. These examples will comprise a private for-profit organization, a nonprofit organization, and an entertainer/businesswoman who live out their core values. These values are central to the philosophies that direct the organization and its followers. These core beliefs of the leader and their organization influence all stakeholders, including partners, clients, employees, and shareholders.

3M Corporation

"At 3M, we apply science in collaborative ways to improve lives daily" (https://www.3m.com/).

3M corporation began in Northern Minnesota over a century ago as a relatively unknown small-scale mining company named *Minnesota Mining and Manufacturing Company*, hence the 3M brand name. Now a modern-day global organization, their vision is *to improve people's daily lives around the world*. Their investment in innovation covering scientific, technical, and marketing advances has produced over sixty thousand products in use today. These products are seen in homes, schools, businesses, hospitals, and many other global industries. They are fully committed to innovative technologies and products that help other organizations advance and improve human life (www.3m.com). 3M has over eighty thousand employees and is known as a global producer of product products that enhance and improve people's lives, no matter location or region.

Their values they have chosen to live by daily demonstrate their commitment to their fellow employees, their investors, and ultimately, the customers they serve day in and day out.

3M believes in six guiding values (www.3m.com):

1. Act with uncompromising honesty and integrity.
2. Satisfy our customers with innovative technology and superior quality, value, and service.

3. Provide our investors an attractive return through sustainable, global growth.
4. Respect our social and physical environment around the world.
5. Value and develop employees' diverse talents, initiative, and leadership.
6. Earn the admiration of all those associated with 3M worldwide.

Their behaviors and actions are guided by their corporate vision and these six fundamental values. They hold honesty and integrity, key servant leadership characteristics, in high regard across the entire organization. 3M takes satisfaction in their high integrity and a law-abiding reputation, including their commitment to protecting the environment, achieving economic success, and practicing social responsibility (www.3m.com).

How does 3M maintain its position as a highly innovative global organization in today's ever-competitive marketplace? 3M invests in Knowledge Management. They utilize a "wide range of Knowledge Management systems"[58] to remain competitive and relevant in the global marketplace arena. 3M. They believe that if people are willing to share knowledge is a cultural benefit that will advance 3M and keep their competitive advantage. This is a primary core value at 3M. The organization "sees Knowledge Management more as a cultural and organizational issue than a technological one."[59] In tandem, they invest in the future generations of 3M employees (leaders and followers) through their commitments and purposeful actions in education, community programs, and environmental initiatives such as Worldskills, Frontline Sales Initiative, Young Scientist Challenge, 3M Visiting Wizards, Higher Education, Community, ad Humanitarian Aid (www.3m.com). These behaviors and actions all align to their values. Here employees must have several of their per-

---

[58] Brand, 17.
[59] Brand, 17.

sonal or individual values in congruence with these organizational values to be successful. In addition, these values also align to servant leadership's virtuous constructs of love, empowerment, altruism, vision, trust, and service to others for their good and benefit.

However, 3M did experience resistance and struggled with bringing the entire workforce together as one. The challenges they faced were a traveling sales team always on the road, a unionized and non-unionized workforce, varying ages of employees spanning from new hires to employees approaching retirement. Their solution was called "We Are 3M," an all-in-one program that produced safety awards, sales incentives, and years of service awards, which were combined and converted into points towards items of their choice. According to 3M Talent Solutions Manager Marnie McKerlie, "The *We Are 3M* program has become part of our culture and helps establish the importance of employee performance and peer recognition in our organization" (www.3m.com). For the first time, employees had the opportunity to give peer-to-peer recognition, which further strengthened their organizational value system and met the individual value needs of the employee. This solution increased employee engagement by seven percent with a ninety-nine percent participation rate in the program. The group that most benefited was the field-based employees who provided superior service to 3M customers. 3M employees daily live out the values of the 3M organization.

The Salvation Army

"ONE ARMY: We see a God-raised, Spirit-filled Army for the 21st century—convinced of our calling, moving forward together" (www.salvationarmy.org).

The Salvation Army is a global organization that is part of the universal Christian Church. Its foundational principles are based on biblical principles for living a life in service, modeling the servant leadership of Jesus Christ. The organization basis its purpose on the love of God with a mission to evangelize the gospel to meet human needs to all people across the globe. The Salvation Army began in 1852 by William Booth and his family from England who chose to spread the gospel to the poor, needy, hungry, destitute, and homeless (www.salvationarmy.org). This eventually grew to a huge volunteer organization and is now a global organization with several thousand employees and volunteers touching people in remote regions and locations that had never heard the gospel. The Salvation Army meets human needs, assists over twenty-three million Americans year over year, serves in over 130 countries, and has over one and a half million members. The current services they provide include disaster relief, rehabilitation, care for the elderly, engagement in the community, and fighting human trafficking. They recently joined an Arizona university program to provide "emergency economic aid for low-income families to pay high-cost electricity bills,"[60] combining efforts to combat those who are destitute in their finances.

While their efforts are still considered evangelic, their focus has changed to more the improvement for the total person, further aligning themselves to servant leadership, which is a complete focus on the follower. Their core values are the following:

1. Passion
2. Compassion
3. Bravery
4. Uplifting Spirit
5. Trustworthiness

These values also align with the individuals who serve in the Salvation Army. This organization is seen in the public on the streets providing for the needy or collecting money and other resources to help the needy. They have storefronts providing basic human needs at reduced costs such as clothing, food, and other basic services while spreading the gospel of Jesus Christ. Those who serve others through the Salvation Army, offer hope and a future to those under privileged or destitute. Servant leadership characteristics of empathy, healing,

---

[60] Zhao, Dickson, Thornton, Solis, and Wentz, 1.

awareness, conceptualization, foresight, stewardship, and building community[61] completely align with the Salvation Army's values.

Dolly Parton

"I've always loved being from where I am, and having the folks that I've had" (www.dollyparton.com).

Dolly Parton (born January 19, 1946) is an American country music singer, businesswoman, songwriter, actress, author, humanitarian, and businesswoman. Here core values shaped who she is today and her achievements throughout her life. She grew up in a low-income family in the Appalachia mountains of Tennessee, rising to stardom by building an entertainment empire based on grit, family values, and a constant smile that attracted many followers for over sixty years. Her consistent attitude and optimism for a brighter future was evident in her life, similar to servant leaders seeking the best for others and a hope for a better tomorrow. Dolly's most favorite and iconic saying is "if you want the rainbow, you gotta put up with the rain!"

Dolly credits her values from her youth in the Great Smoky Mountains, where she never was ashamed of her family or people from where she grew up, no matter how poor or condition they were in. She says, "It's [My upbringing] made me what I am. It's that spiritual base; it's that family; love of family; it's just that simple life, feeling like part of nature."[62] *Harvard Business Review*[63] highlights three leadership traits of Dolly Parton:

1. Giving. Leaders seek the good in others and offer themselves for their success.
2. Forgiving. Forgive those who have wronged you and ask forgiveness for those you have wronged. Grudges cause ani-

---

[61] Joseph and Winston, 1.
[62] (Teague 2015).
[63] Harvard Business Review.

mosity and only spreads to others, driving poor results or adverse outcomes.

3. Loving. Have a strong desire or passion for thier work. This becomes contagious amongst others and contributes to increased performance and growth.[64]

Dolly's leadership characteristics and values align with servant leadership's virtues of altruism, humility, and love of people.[65]

Insights on Examples

Values drive behavior that works to satisfy needs and, ultimately the wants of individuals: our values, both individual and organizational, orient leaders and followers toward ways of accomplishing goals. A leader's values determine thier criteria or standards of what is important to them. Values serve the ideals people become passionate about and desire to achieve for themselves and others. Most people wish to make a difference and seek purpose in thier lives which dictates thier terminal and instrumental values. Terminal values are ideals can be fulfilled in individuals lives through the application of instrumental values, behavioral, and purposeful acts towards a desired goal or end-state. When leaders invest into followers and help them move up Maslow's hierarchy beyond the phycological, safety, and social needs toward self-esteem and then self-actualization, they are changing their lives for their benefit and others good. This change can lead to future servant leaders seeking to reciprocate this behavior to others, becoming a multiplier effect.

How do leaders and organizations know they are living out their values for others to see and mimic? Leaders should continually validate their behaviors and actions against their values, even if it is not in their best interests. A value can either attract or distance people from a leader and their organization. Values need to be continually

---

[64] (Baldoni 2008).

[65] Patterson.

validated and displayed for others to see and experience for a leader or organization is to stay relevant and achieve its expected outcomes.

An interview with Mr. Robin Manning,
retired electric power utility executive

Mr. Manning has led thousands of utility employees over a forty-year career for Duke Energy, the Tennessee Valley Authority, and the Electric Power Research Institute. Though he has retired, he still serves as an active member of the North American Electric Reliability Corporation. Currently, Mr. Manning serves as President of One Heart Global Ministries, an Ecuadorian-focused mission organization. Rob and his family reside in Charlotte, North Carolina, and are active in his church, Hickory Grove Baptist Church, serving as a deacon, teaching Sunday school, and an avid singer in the church choir.

Who is the organization you worked for or served, and in what capacity? There are four distinct organizations I worked for, each with very different issues. Many have similar core values, but how those values adapt and change with external factors is different. I worked for thirty years at Duke Energy, a very large electric utility. At Duke, I held many vice president positions, ending my career as the vice president of Field Operations for the Carolinas. I left Duke to join the Tennessee Valley Authority (TVA) as the executive vice president of Power System Operations. I stayed at TVA for six years and went to join the Electric Power Research Institute (EPRI) as VP of Transmission and Distribution, where I worked three years before retiring. Since 2010, I have also served as the president of One Heart Global Ministries, a Christian-based nonprofit.

What are the core values of your organization? Duke Energy's values are similar to most corporation values. Almost all companies embrace similar foundational values. Duke started with Safety, then embraced employee interaction through "Caring." Most organizations have "Integrity" as a core value, so did Duke. Also, "Respect." A few that I saw uniquely expressed at Duke were Openness (targeting creativity and innovation) and Passion (striving for excellence). TVA values are very similar, Safety, Integrity, Inclusion, and Service.

Service applies more specifically to TVA as it is a fully public organization—owned by the public and operating entirely in an open general environment. EPRI is a more straightforward company. EPRI is a nonprofit organization to support the overall utility industry. It is a small organization of about eight hundred folks—many of which are experts in their fields. There are many doctorates and degrees at EPRI. Because of the research mission, values were very pointed toward innovation and creativity—since that was the main product EPRI marketed. EPRI values included integrity, objectivity, and public benefit. As for One Heart Global Ministries (OHGM), we have never documented our values, but the values are more distinctly Christian as a Christian organization. I would suggest OHGM values are Love for one another, Faith in our Lord Jesus, and Charity in bringing donations to where they are most needed to serve Christ.

Do you see these values changing at all, and if so, how? Not at OHGM. Love, faith, and charity are eternal. I have also seen EPRI hold pretty fast to values because they undergird the organization's mission, with a specific focus on creating and innovating. However, both TVA and Duke are undergoing change that parallels the changing environment in which they do business. TVA is always in a unique position as its board members are selected by the sitting president, and its internal budgets are subject to congressional approval. As such, the winds of politics tend to nudge TVA slightly left or right of their traditional center. Even so, TVA tries to hold fast to its core roots while appeasing the powers that be. That means safety and service are pretty solid, but integrity and inclusion might look just a little different depending on who is in charge. For example, when TVA recently decided to outsource a sizeable number of IT folks, President Trump fired two board members and did everything he could to fire the CEO. By contrast, consider the position of inclusion in the Biden administration compared to the Trump administration, and you can see the challenge the organization faces.

Nonetheless, they try very hard to hold the line. At Duke Energy, changes there are more subtle yet metamorphic when looking backward. Duke is an investor-owned company and does most internal business out of the public eye. As such, their values slowly adapt to track the times. This doesn't affect the mainstays, like Safety and Respect, but impacts inclusion, caring, openness, and even innovation. As society shifts toward a different definition of inclusion, the definition narrows, along with its acceptance of alternative thoughts. Over time this wears down the edges of pushback and results in a more subservient mindset. In other words, people tend not to push against the edges because the consequences of being accused of being outside values are severe. As a result, innovation drops creativity drops. On the positive side, behavior becomes more predictable and aligned. It is truly a fine line between defining and managing aligned behavior and accepting and encouraging creativity along the edge.

How does your organization reflect and live out these values? For OHGM, it is simple, all we do is ministry. We don't embrace anything other than sharing Christ and serving his people. There is no glory outside the glory of Christ. EPRI also has a simple enough model that its mission and values are also its product. They cannot help but align because it is what they do by definition. As for the other large utilities, this is more of a struggle. TVA fights it openly in a public way. People are different. Employees are different. They have different opinions, they may or may not embrace the way the wind blows, and they often manifest their thoughts in their behavior. For TVA, this sometimes happens in the newspaper or television. Duke has more control because they operate outside the public eye, but sometimes this catches them unaware—as with the ash-pond spill a few years back. Contrast their response to the TVA ash-pond response of a couple of years before. TVA immediately opened itself to the public, and the arguments and solutions all played out publicly. By contrast, Duke was considerably more insular and fought a more drawn-out and complex battle as a result. In the end, I doubt either approach changed the outcome very much. In all cases, organizational values are lived out by the employees that represent the organizations. When the employees know and embrace the values, then that is what you get. When the employees don't get it, or don't like it, you most certainly do *not* get the values you might state publically.

What would you recommend to leaders and organizations when developing their core values in pursuit of forming a dynamic and resil-

ient organization? How can they sustain them, especially in turbulent/ challenging or in times of crisis? This is a great question! The places I have seen the most remarkable success are aligned mission, values, objectives, and products. Everything has to reflect the same purpose. It doesn't work to hold a session and brainstorm core values. Core values are already known, already being used in any organization. One doesn't need a process to think up the core values you would *like* to have; one needs a strategy to capture the ones you already reflect. If you want to *change* them, that is a different challenge. At one organization, we had a consultant lead several sessions to identify a really neat list of values. They read very well, and they resonated each and every one. *But* they did not reflect how we went about doing our work, and they failed to catch hold. A sustaining value is a value that is not influenced by a political or social issue, but is underpinned by a moral or business fundamental. Almost every organization has a core value of integrity because doing business without integrity is simply not sustainable. This is the importance of a biblically-based perspective, as the fundamentals of right and wrong have been defined for thousands of years and have persevered through the most difficult of times. Select values that resonate with what you are already doing and line up with what you want to deliver. Choose values that augment right versus wrong. Select values that apply uniformly even as social norms change. For example, respect and inclusion is always the right thing to do. One might adjust how or who is included as societal norms shift, but the foundation of respect and inclusion is always right.

I believe much of this circles back to the concept of servant leadership. Leading is not about defining for people right and wrong. Leading is about embedding right and wrong within people. It is more a function of demonstrating with consistency the behavior you wish others to show. Servant leadership pulls the best out of people; it identifies the unique qualifications and skills God has planted within them and allows those skills and qualities to shine. Servant leadership is shepherding. It is rounding up sheep, loving them, and guiding them to the right place without ever having to pick them up and move them yourself. Even if they sometimes aggravate the mess out of you. Servant Leaders let others thrive, so the overall objective is achieved. Servant leaders live their values in a way that others want to follow. This is true of "selecting" core values. Our core values are already selected. God has placed them on our hearts. If you want to document values that sustain you in the worst of times, pull them from your heart, not from a PowerPoint deck.

Practical Application

Where can a leader begin to identify, define, and live out their values both as individuals and the organization they serve? What steps can they take now and ensure their values and the culture they form to stay relevant and dynamic in today's fast-paced and ever-changing workplace? Those organizations that have clear, concise, and a shared belief and meaning of values will significantly impact every facet of their company.

Determining and living one's values

For a leader or a follower to determine their values, they must focus on both terminal (goals, objectives, end-states) and instrumental (modes of conduct, behaviors, actions, lifestyle) values and how they work together. Where does a leader start? How can they determine these values to lead effectively? The following paragraphs outline a three-step process of identifying and defining individual values.

To begin, look at Table 1 terminal values and determine which three to five you identify with. This is not all-inclusive but more of a beginning exercise to start a leader down the right path in achieving value realization. Then take time to define and write down what that terminal value means to you as a leader, such as equality, peace, self-respect, and freedom. For example, equality may mean acknowledging all people from a moral, social, and respectful position similar to Agapoe love (Patterson 2003). How can these terminal values be chosen to benefit others? What groups organizations can you join and contribute to live out these values? Frequently evaluate and determine if your terminal values change over time, meaning are you adding any others or possibly removing some given your current beliefs and desires to make a change for the greater good of all people?

For instrumental values, apply the same exercise to determine your position, behaviors, and actions to support terminal values. This requires frequent assessment and application to drive your terminal values. Determine what specific behaviors will support and further strengthen your terminal values.

Determining and living out one's organizational values

Determining an organization's values requires a comparative evaluation of the organization's culture. A leader must examine how these values drive the mission and vision of the organization, forming its unique and purposeful culture.[66] The exercise discussed in the individual value realization can also be applied at the organizational level. The following steps will help a leader in defining and living out the organization's values:

1. Define short, specific, and easy-to-remember values. For example, many organizations believe in respect for the individual and is commonly understood amongst several nations such as the United States and the United Kingdom[67] and global organizations such as International Business Machines (www.ibm.com) and UNESCO, the United Nations Educational, Scientific and Cultural Organization (www.unesco.org).
2. Keep them specific and directly aligned to an organization's mission and vision with relevancy to what the organization does or produces, reflecting its culture.
3. Align values with both internal and external goals. This provides a bridge and drives the organization's culture.

---

[66] Schein and Schein, 344.
[67] (Hofstede, Hofstede and Minkov 2010).

When people see the greater good the organization is trying to achieve, such as climate control, pollution reduction, and a healthier global population, they often line up quickly behind these efforts, supporting these terminal values. Customers will also begin to trust your leadership and the organization when they see the good a leader and their organization is trying to bring forth.

Once these values are established, ensure they are embedded throughout the organization such as on the company website, on walls in the hallways, on letterhead, and repeated during typical internal meetings with all employees and stakeholders present. For example, one of Microsoft's fundamental values is trust. Their statement to their customers with their cloud technologies is "Microsoft runs on trust" (www.microsoft.com). It is critical for Microsoft to continually espouse that value within its culture for all leaders and followers to live out in all internal and external (customers, stakeholders, partners) interactions.

Organizational Culture Instrument (OCIA) and Competing Values Framework

Academic authors and organizational research Professors Cameron and Quinn designed the OCIA and the Competing Values Framework,[68] believing a solid and relevant organizational culture will drive organizational success and effectiveness. This framework is one of several that will help a servant leader assess their culture and identify areas of change and improvement as required. Culture is comprised of people's values, beliefs, and norms forming the organization. These values guide how people relate to each other and how they respond and adapt to the outside environment. Studies have shown that when both the individual and organizational values align to a shared culture, performance increases, profitability rises,

---

[68] (Cameron and Quinn 2011).

and organizational effectiveness is achieved. The goal of the OCIA is to align an organization's culture with its strategic direction. The cultural profile from this assessment displays an organization's current culture and the desired future-state culture. The OCIA reveals differences between the two cultures and determines if the organization's culture is congruent (in agreement). The culture profile highlights current values, behaviors, and potential changes for organizational success and effectiveness. Cameron and Quinn[69] provide four culture types, clan, adhocracy, market, and hierarchy. Called the Competing Values Framework:

1. The clan (collaborate) culture emphasizes a family-like environment where teamwork, encouragement, and employee development are prevalent throughout the organization. The atmosphere is often characterized as a friendly workplace where leaders encourage team participation, consensus, and loyalty to the organization.

2. The Adhocracy (create) culture focuses on an ever-changing environment stressing entrepreneurship, innovation, taking a risk trying new ideas, and willingness to accept the failure of an idea or program. This environment allows for dynamic change and the implementation of new concepts quickly. Typical organizations that emphasize adhocracy are technology, aerospace, and consulting organizations.

3. The Market (compete) culture emphasizes the external environment in a goal-oriented and hard-driving environment to complete ordinary tasks and produce results quickly. Success is demonstrated through the results produced, with minimal concern to internal organization impact.

4. The Hierarchy (control culture) focuses on structure, rules, and authority within the organization. Governance and formal policies prevail throughout the entire structure.

---

[69] (Cameron and Quinn 2011).

Most organizations with a strong hierarchy culture provide step-by-step guidelines with slight deviation or changing of rules without formal approval.[70]

Creating A Learning Culture

While both individual and organizational values come together to form a unique culture, what does it mean to have a learning culture? Why is this important? Today's organizations face continual global social, economic, and political competition that was not present some thirty years ago. Culture plays such a critical role in all organizations to remain relevant and thrive in today's marketplace. To not only survive but thrive, leaders must build an always learning culture. Microsoft CEO Satya Nadella says, "Don't be a know it all, be a learn it all."[71]

First, the learning culture must be proactive in identifying problems early on and proactively solving them before becoming consequential to the organization. Through scenario planning, problems can be preemptively identified and quickly assessed for the potential impact and risk remediation.[72] According to Schein, "active problem-solving leads to learning, thereby setting an appropriate example for other members of the organization."[73] This will then motivate others to follow the example and create a learning culture.

Second, each organization member must believe and live out an "always learning" personal value, which will become an organizational value. Back in the 1980s, Digital Equipment Corporation (DEC) held a core value of innovation but suffered from a commitment to continual learning. The leader and follower must seek feedback along their journey and be willing to pivot as needed. The key for any organization is the willingness to try new ideas and inno-

---

[70] (Cameron and Quinn 2011).

[71] (S. Nadella 2017).

[72] (Hines 2006).

[73] Schein and Schein, 344.

vation through learning, accepting shortfalls and failings while pursuing excellence in service to one another.

Third, a learning culture must assume and believe that both the leader and follower lead with goodness and seek to do good for others. Goodness comes from the inner core of a person and by nature, seeks good in others.[74] Pursuing goodness in others aligns with servant leadership characteristics of building community, the approach of creating and living out shared values for all to see and embrace.[75] The leader must belief that all people are willing to learn and ready to change as they grow in their skillsets and abilities to become better every day. Ultimately, a leader must always show a positive attitude to all they interact with, including those who report to them, their peers, and their leaders for a learning culture to thrive.

---

[74] (Borcarnea, et al. 2018).

[75] (Joseph and Winston 2003).

CHAPTER 4

The Power of a Leader's Vision

Vision in terms of servant leadership is about focusing on the follower and how they will impact the future. The leader invests in their followers to ensure they are growing, developing, and helping others achieve a future state where both the organization and the individual benefit. The following paragraphs will provide (1) additional meanings and definitions of vision, (2) discuss why vision is vital to the leader, the follower, and the organization, (3) the importance of a shared vision, and (4) finally, how service to others will strengthen and develop a resilient vision.

When the word *vision* comes to mind, thoughts of a future state and what it may look and feel like for the organization and the individual begin to emerge. According to Ackermann and Eden, "vision provides the motivation to do things but little help with how to decide and behave in relation to specific issues."[76] Another example of vision is identifying the group and what they aspire to achieve or accomplish over some time. For a vision to have meaning and not just a goal measured by a metric, such as increasing sales by twenty percent in one year, it must have a logical understanding and touch people's hearts and souls. Vision inspires and creates hope for

---

[76] Ackermann and Eden, 40.

a better future.[77] A leader castes a brighter future for themselves and the organization, especially in service to others. The vision begins the adventure through a journey often met with frequent struggles and setbacks, yet, there are periods of joy and achievement sprinkled throughout towards the final destination. Examples of visions that communicate meaning and inspire followers will be discussed later.

A servant leader's vision should align with the individuals' core values that make up the organization's core values. These values are often shared by followers, such as a family or clan-like environment, highly ethical and moral treatment, equality for all, and growth. A servant leader seeks a better world by casting a vision for their followers to align these values and join in the vision for their personal development and for the entire organization to excel. However, at times, the individual and organizational values may not align completely, resulting in frustration, resulting in poor performance for both the individual and the organization.

Servant leaders must always be forward-thinking and looking to the follower and how they can help them continually improve and grow. Most importantly, how is the leader serving their people for growth and maturity to occur? Are they building the right culture and environment to serve as a launching pad for follower growth and self-actualization? These questions should be routinely asked several times throughout the year, not just at annual organizational health and performance reviews. Vision and servant leadership are closely related to each other because a leader "needs to have a sense for the unknowable and be able to foresee the unforeseeable."[78] A servant leader can dramatically impact their followers' work and personal lives through service, inspiring them to serve others and vision for others to join in and achieve fulfillment.

What does a vision do for servant leaders, the followers, and the entire organization? Why is vision so important to develop early on in an organization, and should it be continually monitored for

---

[77] (Engstrom 1976).
[78] Greenleaf, 21–22.

changes and improvement? First of all, vision provides clarity. It also helps the leader and his organization define what they would like to create and what they desire to accomplish. According to Patterson, vision provides "a way of looking at what one wants to be, or how he should be.[79] The servant-leader can see the vision as a clear picture of the future, which may be invisible to the follower at first. Vision helps the servant leader and their followers achieve the desired state because of clarified values and beliefs, bringing them together. Vision begins with the end state in mind.[80] When a leader keeps vision at the forefront of the organization, they develop discernment for their future planning and direction. However, equally important to a leader's vision, understanding and grasping the current reality serves as a base and trajectory for casting a vision into the future. When a servant leader enters a meeting, they should always ask, "What is the vision and what is the strategy?" These two questions help clarify everyone's understanding of the group's identity and future state. The second part, strategy, is about the agreement and executing those priorities to achieve the organization's purpose.[81]

Second, vision creates momentum, vigor, and energy in the organization. Vision provides a means of assessing progress towards a goal or destination. The ultimate destination may not be wholly defined; however, the focus should be qualifying and quantifying advancement over time. Jesus Christ gave a vision to his followers to inspire and motivate them in their calling as disciples, "As Jesus walked beside the Sea of Galilee, he saw Simon and his brother Andrew casting a net into the lake, for they were fishermen. 'Come, follow me,' Jesus said, 'and I will send you out to fish for people.' At once they left their nets and followed him."[82] Servant leaders build consensus, using idealized inspiration and motivation,[83] leading the

---

[79] Patterson, 5.

[80] (Covey 1989).

[81] (Deterding 2016).

[82] Mk. 1:16–18.

[83] (Conger 1999).

way and helping followers see and realize their progress in growing their unique talents and gifts.

Third, vision creates a focus for the follower and the organization they serve. A shared vision brings purpose and meaning into the daily activities in pursuit of goals and objectives. A servant leader should focus on how they can identify and strengthen each follower's unique talents and abilities in shaping the future, yet keeping a continual service mindset to them. Fourth, vision creates accountability, responsibility, and commitment in service to everyone. Castiglione states accountability is a "principle according to which a person or institution is responsible for a set of duties and can be required to give an account of their fulfillment to an authority that is in a position to issue rewards or punishment."[84] This area of a vision statement defines each individual's scope and expectation as to their contributions to the organization's success. When followers commit and deliver in their work, not only is success achieved for the individual, but the organization as a whole benefit, and the vision becomes fulfilled. Again, a shared vision aligns each individual's vision and contributes immensely to the organization's overall performance. The servant-leader is responsible for vision creation and definition. However, a vision attainment can only be achieved through the alignment, inclusion, and the embracing of the follower's vision based on their values.

Fourth, vision directs and influences the service virtue of servant leadership. While the number one goal of a servant leader is to serve others, their focus is to change the follower for their greater good and purpose, becoming more servant-like.[85] For example, Jesus Christ saught to influence and transform followers through his acts of servanthood to pursue his Kingdom vision for all to align and continue in His mission. However, Jesus came not to serve humanity but out of obedience and service to his "Heavenly Father."[86] The vision then becomes a shared vision across the entire organization.

---

[84] (Castiglione 2012).
[85] (Sendjaya 2015).
[86] Sendjaya, 106.

The servant-leader focuses on service to help their followers grow, strengthen, and achieve their abilities and ultimately become servant leaders to others.

Fifth, "vision creates volunteers."[87] When a leader makes the vision extremely clear, simple to understand and comprehend, and in such a compelling way, followers automatically desire to join in and become a part of the vision's momentum. "A compelling vision is the reason why millions of individuals give nearly five hours each week to nonprofit organizations."[88] The follower sees their contributions moving the organization towards vision attainment.

Sixth, vision ensures that the organization is not dependent on a single individual or group. In other words, the vision continues beyond the founders of the organization. The vision must outlast the leader for the organization to continue. A servant leader keeps this in check with his followers through leadership succession to continue in service for vision continuance.

Vision Examples in Leaders and the Workplace

The following section will provide several examples of both a leader's vision and an organization's vision to demonstrate how a future state of being is created and shared with others to pursue attainment.

Nelson Mandela

"Vision without action is just a dream, action without vision just passes the time, vision with action can change the world" (Marketwire 2013).

Nelson Mandela (1918–2013), former president of South Africa (1994–1999), was a visionary leader[89] and a world-renowned

---

[87] Sendjaya, 106.
[88] Sendjaya, 107.
[89] Johnson and Hackman, 269.

servant leader.[90] He envisioned a South African nation where all people would have equal rights and vote for the government officials of their choice. His life's vision sought to eradicate racism and establish a constitutional democracy for South Africa. Where did this vision for changing a nation come from? How did President Mandela implement his vision resulting in the removal of apartheid in South Africa?

Nelson Mandela devoted his entire life to all South Africans' freedom, no matter race or culture, against apartheid. Because of his beliefs, he was imprisoned for twenty-seven years before becoming president. His vision for a free and fully democratized South Africa came from his years of fighting within the prison for all people's rights. During this time, he grew his faith and found his purpose through the "African spiritual ethic, Ubuntu."[91] Ubuntu is a behavior or an act towards others as a moral duty to support and help everyone. While people have the right and ability to advance themselves, developing their individual Ubuntu, there is a natural innate desire and passion for growing spiritually within one's community, where everyone benefits. Ubuntu aligns with the servant leadership virtues of humility, altruism, trust, and Agapoe love of others. "Mandela found that the power of Ubuntu, the inner core of every person's humanity, could move mountains."[92] This approach to servant leadership brings together the notion of generosity and sincere humanity. While Ubuntu has many variations, especially in the sub-Sharan region, the core concept is generally understood and practiced, thus helping President Mandela build his shared vision.

President Mandela purposely and perfectly aligned his vision with the people of South Africa, resulting in the "global anti-apartheid movement,"[93] from 1988 to 1994, based on the values of the people selecting government officials through democratic elections and fair and equitable human treatment of all people. After his release from prison, his first public speech shared his vision as a servant leader

---

[90] Ferch, Spears, McFarland, and Carey, 218.
[91] Oppenheim, 369.
[92] Oppenheim, 370.
[93] Olesen, 34.

for the people of South Africa, giving tribute to those who sacrificed their lives in the fight for freedom. "I stand here before you not as a prophet but as a humble servant of you, the people. Your tireless and heroic sacrifices have made it possible for me to be here today. I, therefore, place the remaining years of my life in your hands."[94] Mandela used this speech to show himself as a humble man seeking service to the South African nation for their greater good as a nation, espousing moral and ethical behavior, humbleness, and self-sacrifice for others to benefit. This speech and many others catapulted him into an instant global public icon, leading the way for his vision and creating a shared vision for all South Africans to be realized and attained through Ubuntu.

During his later years, Mandela reflected on his life as a servant leader. His desire for personal freedom and individual rights while in prison transformed into a vision for all South Africans. Mandela posited, "Freedom is indivisible… It was during those long and lonely years that my hunger for the freedom of my own people became a hunger for the freedom of all people, white and black."[95] His vision of individual freedom and the eventual freedom of all Mission South Africans transformed a nation through hs vision of change and hope for a better future.

Satya Nadella, CEO of Microsoft

Vision: "To empower every person and every organization on the planet to achieve more." https://www.microsoft.com/en-us/about).

On February 4, 2014, Satya Nadella became Microsoft's third Chief Executive Officer (CEO) for Microsoft. While an unlikely candidate for the CEO role, he was an insider with over twenty-two years at Microsoft, rising in several leadership roles. One of his first acts as CEO was to send out what is commonly known as his "vision

---

[94] *New York Times.*
[95] Mandela, 624.

memo."[96] This email, known as "a rite of passage," addressed all employees and detailed his vision for Microsoft and its future. This email was labeled, "Stay Nadella—Microsoft's New CEO," which spoke of his vision for computing technology and how it will evolve into a digital transformation of all organizations worldwide. The primary mission and vision of Microsoft from his predecessor Bill Gates and Steve Ballmer aspired to have "a PC on every desk and home," pivoted to "to empower every person and every organization on the planet to achieve more" (https://www.microsoft.com/en-us/about). His bold and ambitious vision laid out the plan and course of Microsoft for the ensuing years. Empowerment, a primary servant leadership virtue, is built into his vision, representing a vital objective of the organization and its strategic direction to what it seeks to achieve. Empowerment in this regard speaks of building communities, surpassing expectations, and including every person within and outside of Microsoft. According to Nadella, the initial vision has, in large part, had been achieved. The new course forward was to unlock the imagination, seek new innovative ideas, and solve those challenges once not thought possible.

Nadella joined Microsoft early on in his professional career because he wanted to be part of an organization that could change the world for all people's betterment. In his prior years at Microsoft, he faced a difficult era of growing bureaucracy and infighting amongst various teams. The colossal behemoth could not pivot to market and customer demands. He realized that Microsoft's culture had to change and re-align its values with a sense of meaning in purpose for everyone who comes to work, day after day. He wanted to have employees return to the days of innovation, ideation, creativity, and ultimately, "to make a difference in the world."[97] Nadella introduced the concept of "growth mindset,"[98] changing the culture, whereas everyone contributes to this notion. "A growth mindset is all about

---

[96] (McGregor 2014).

[97] Mandela, 2.

[98] Nadella and Euchner, 12.

going from know-it-alls to learn-it-alls."[99] This paradigm shift would take time, but within two years, the fruits of his labor and those aligned to Microsoft's new vision began to yield fruit in the form of improved market penetration and increased stock price.

His vision castes a broad scope with clarity with a sense of purpose and meaning for all to join in, including all people, no matter location or origin. His vision guides the organization's strategy "to build best-in-class platforms and productivity services for this mobile-first, cloud-first world. Its three ambitions relate to reinventing productivity and business procedures, building an intelligent cloud platform, and create more personal computing."[100] What drives this vision and strategy? Culture. Nadella realized the culture had to change for the vision to be ingrained in the culture. While not specifically called out, this vision directly aligns with servant leadership's virtues of love, humility, empowerment, and altruism. His focus had always been to change the world for the greater good of all and create a future that will benefit those who have yet to be born into it.[101] His futuristic vision speaks of optimism, hope, and challenges that lie ahead for those who seek a better, caring, and empathetic world for all people.

United Nations International Children's Emergency Fund (UNICEF)

Vision: "To create a world where the rights of every child are realized" (https://www.unicef.org).

The United Nations International Children's Fund, called UNICEF,[102] provides relief aid to children and their mothers struggling to survive. This humanitarian effort started after World War II in 1946 as a temporary relief organization providing essential food and clothing to the children of Europe and China. Eventually, UNICEF became a member of the United Nations with a presence now in over

---

[99] Nadella and Euchner, 12.
[100] Hopping, 1.
[101] (Gurgaon 2014).
[102] (Morris 2015).

"190 countries, advocating for maternal and child health and welfare while still upholding its original commitment to provide emergency relief aid to children and mothers in conflict regions."[103] After World War II, UNICEF became aligned with the United Nations (UN) purpose in maintaining peace in the world and meeting the survival needs of children and their mothers to improve health and education. This agency is commonly known throughout the globe as a highly recognized social welfare organization. Their services include immunizations for disease prevention, HIV prevention, improving nutrition for children and their mothers, educational opportunities, and urgent aid and relief after a natural disaster.

UNICEF's vision "to create a world where the rights of every child are realized" is forward-looking and all-inclusive. This vision seeks to protect and support all children's rights through adolescence, advocating for their rights and future well-being. The vision statement also has global influence and touch, impacting every child that identifies with this circumstance. While not specifically stated, the mothers of the children are considered part of UNICEF's vision and purpose. However, there was a change in policy due to the impact of "a powerful Western women's movement that it changes its views on women and their role in the care of children"[104] This change brought UNICEF to realize that children's rights differed from women's, especially those seeking educational opportunities to improve their social and financial status. UNICEF had to rethink its approach to a region or location instead of assuming the needs and expectations are the same across the globe.

UNICEF's core values encompass respect, integrity, care, and love for all people, similar to the virtues of servant leadership. The focus on complete and absolute care for every child who needs protection and fundamental human rights is evident in their culture and way of life. UNICEF sees these core values as a way of life, uniting the organization to pursue its vision and execute a strategy to deliver

---

[103] Morris, 1.
[104] Morris, 8.

excellent care and service to all. UNICEF also continues to maintain its status as a prominent global organization in its pursuit of ensuring the fair and equitable rights of children and their mothers.

Insights on Examples

These vision statements demonstrate the critical attributes required of a servant leader and the organization's attributes in service to others. They also all bring forth the clarity of their future and their organization's purpose. They also create passion and excitement to pursue positive change globally, solving complex issues for today and the future. Finally, these visions have a complete focus on the follower, developing into a shared vision with servant leadership virtues encouraging people to join in to change the world for everyone. A servant leader must have the vision at the forefront with everyone who engages and encounters their organization, driving its purpose, intent, and actions. The vision should excite and empower everyone to join in the vision. A leader must be ever vigilant in their display and practice in achieving and fulfilling the vision.

An interview with Scott Woods, chief of staff and director of Special Projects of Samaritan's Feet

Samaritan's Feet is a 501(c)(3) organization that serves and inspires hope in children by providing shoes as the foundation to a spiritual and healthy life. Scott has built his career around helping companies unlock their potential and growth through optimizing their operational and financial processes, creating a culture of excellence, and building a solid foundation for maximum profit. He is a coach, consultant, speaker, investor, and small business owner. He has had the privilege of working with some of the most influential companies in the Charlotte, North Carolina, metro area.

What does the vision of "Samaritan's Feet serves and inspires hope in children by providing shoes as the foundation to a spiritual and healthy life resulting in the advancement of education and economic opportunities" *do for Samaritan's Feet and the people you serve? Why was this chosen?*

As with any vision statement, the goal is to expound on the desired impact the organization wants to have on its customers and in the case of a nonprofit, the community at large. At its core, the vision of Samaritan's Feet is to inspire hope through the gift of shoes. That hope is for a better tomorrow—a tomorrow that is filled with opportunities and anticipation, not of struggle but the prosperity of both a physical and spiritual nature. We know shoes are a necessary element for both school and work in developing countries. We also know that new shoes are a symbol of dignity for those in the US and in developed countries. Children with new(er) shoes walk with their heads held higher and with confidence that they are looked upon as more of equals.

Why is this vision important to Samaritan's Feet? A vision statement guides the mission tactics for any organization. Without a properly developed and delineated vision, an organization will often experience a drift in its mission. This mission drift, a scattered approach because of a poorly explained vision, can cause irreparable harm to an organization's credibility and effectiveness. However, if an organization and its executives know without a doubt the desired impact (vision), it can effectively create the tactics (mission) to get to that desired goal. At Samaritan's Feet, we work very hard to constantly vet potential opportunities and program ideas against the vision statement. It guides the yes/no/maybe decisions and creates a framework for evaluation. We don't do it perfectly by any means. It is a constant battle to ascertain which grants and donor groups to engage with.

How do your staff and volunteers live out the shared vision of Samaritan's Feet? Every employee knows the vision and uses it to guide decisions, as detailed above. We also work hard to reinforce the vision and mission during quarterly (internal) "town hall" meetings and annual staff retreats. Additionally, the staff is encouraged to participate in our outreach events, shoe distributions, fundraising events, and speaking engagements as they feel led. The organization truly empowers the staff to be active spokespeople in their spheres of influence (schools, clubs, businesses).

Do you see the vision of Samaritan's Feet changing in the future, and if so, what do you foresee in that vision? The desired impact (vision) is far more static than the tactics used to reach that impact (mission). While the tactics may change, I don't see the vision changing. I see a potential simplification of the vision statement to inspire hope and foster inspiration, knowing the educational, spiritual, and physical benefits would follow in due course. As the organization continues to grow and adapt to the ever-changing environment, we will undoubtedly find new ways to inspire children and adults to lives of impact through the simple act of service. We will never waiver from the desire to see people live a life focused on helping others achieve their dreams, knowing you never reach alone. Success both individually and corporately is grounded in community and promotes the rising tide that raises all boats.

If you were to advise or consult another leader or organization on vision, what would that be? As I have mentioned previously, vision relates to the desired impact an organization (or individual) wants to have. There are numerous templates and discussions around vision/ mission, but I advise other leaders to think about it in the simplest of terms truly:

Vision = desired impact
Mission = how we get there
Values = guiding principles (or big rocks as I call them)

Keeping these three terms in perspective as leaders work through their organizational initiatives is paramount. Annual strategy, planning, and budget meetings should always include looking through the lens of vision and aligning with mission and values. Once you are rock solid on the VMV, you can make decisions based on that framework. Those decisions are now much easier to promote, get adoption from stakeholders and implement because everyone agrees the decisions align with MVV.

My biggest piece of advice for newer organizations is not neglecting this step in the business planning process. My advice for established businesses is similar—build into your annual planning a review and discussion on MVV.

Practical Application: Building and Sustaining the Vision

So how does a leader create and sustain a vision for themselves and the organization they serve? What approach should a leader take when embarking on creating a vision statement encompassing the key attributes discussed earlier, both in definition and example? The following steps of identifying, developing, setting, sustaining, and releasing a vision will serve as a foundational basis for today's modern leader and their organization.

1. *Vision development: Define, identify, create accountability, and responsibility areas.*

No matter the organization or leadership approach, all visions require a leader to define, identify, and create accountability and responsibility areas for vision development. This method enables a leader to consider their vision and align with the organization, further extending beyond your desires. Next, determine a list of major responsibility areas (MRA) such as family, personal career aspirations, financial, community involvement, physical, spiritual, and most importantly, impact beyond thier sphere of influence that will leave a legacy for others to follow and model. Sendjaya (2015) states, "One of the greatest legacies that you can leave others is a vision that will outlast generations of leaders."[105] The list provided is a short list to jump-start your vision creation and development; this by no means is all inclusive but will guide as a servant leader going down the right path for themselves and the organizations they serve. Take time to prioritize the list and stay committed to the execution of those top three or five. As a leader, develop the initial draft, keep in mind, the list may grow and mirror others, which is fine. As time

---

[105] Sendjaya, 113.

progresses, revisit that list and ask, what has changed, if anything? Has the scope changed? Change and transformation will be discussed in other sections. Note, there are no wrong answers when creating accountability and responsibility areas; remember, this is based upon what the leader believes and foresees for the future. To get started, a leader should write down their thoughts on either a piece of paper or a whiteboard. The leader should ask what their person vision is and how can this be extended beyond themselves, leaving a legacy for others to follow and model. Then expand the vision by incorporating family, friends, colleagues, and people who will give honest feedback. Often, those who take the time to critic a leader's work are the ones who provide the most relevant and impactful feedback. Note, the leader may not have much in common with these critics (political, economic, social). However, they often provide the most relevant and impactful feedback that will strengthen and grow you as a leader.

2. *Define and commit to a vision for each major responsibility area.*

Next, a leader takes each major responsibility area (MRA) and set clear and concise goals to achieve it. Here is where vision becomes action. As a leader, establish and begin to implement specific activities or tasks to fulfill each MRA. Determine how you will measure progress and how you will overcome challenges and setbacks. For example, begin with the people and the environment you serve, are there visible artifacts of the vision in the buildings and collateral? Can the leader's followers and everyone they interact with recite and explain the vision? Ask the followers how they can ensure everyone they interact with will understand and comprehend the vision is either seen in action or word, and communicated. For example, Samaritan's Feet continually promotes images of its staff and volunteers providing shoes and washing children's feet in social media and printed publications. Their website offers the testimony of its CEO Manny Ohonme and his desire to have a good pair of sneakers as a young boy in Nigeria and how this changed his life when he eventually did receive his pair of sneakers. This sneakers' gift carried on through his future vision and passion for providing footwear to others as a global cause. This act of generosity became his life's passion and vision, which is still to this day carried out through all who engage with him and his organization through shoe distribution.

When evaluating and analyzing each MRA, determine one or two goals with specific measurements for achievement. These goals should be categorized and measured over time with expected milestones and completion dates. Don't worry if you fail to meet everyone from your initial draft. See this as a learning opportunity for the future. However, recognize and celebrate those goals that you did achieve success. A leader should set a goal for themself and everyone to recite the vision and articulate its impact to all people, no matter who approaches them. This task could be the first month's goal. Second, within six months of having the vision in place, demonstrate through visible objects and images its presence and influence. In other words, are there banners, logos, and visual markers of your organization's vision? Does your organization's products or services have the vision built into them? Continue this process with each MRA and its strategic goals.

3. *Review and evaluate your vision and strategic goals.*

As time progresses, both the leader's vision and the people they engage with will change. One thing is for sure for all people and organizations; change is continual. The goal of a leader is to ensure that change will further grow and strengthen their ability to lead the organization's people. To start, build a plan for periodic reviews and evaluations of the vision and goals. Some organizations hold two to three executive leadership vision events throughout the calendar year. Churches often hold "vision nights" within their local congregations to gain input and provide where their leadership believes their church is going. Other organizations have in-person and remote "town halls." Note, this should not be a meeting of just receiving and gathering information and exploring possibilities of what the future could be or hold for the organization. Open dialogue and listening of leadership must be present for these vision meetings to be effective. While there are always specific guidelines organizations must follow from a legal obligation, this activity encourages innovation and growth for the leader and their organization. This approach requires all people involved and committed to the vision to have an open mind and a willingness to try something new, letting go and leaving their "comfort zone." So set specific checkpoints with the leadership team and the organization, staying committed to regularly holding these.

4. *Engage your organization and seek professional guidance through outside counsel.*

Your vision creation and implementation will be one of the first acts of displaying your leadership. It makes no difference if the vision is for a large audience of several thousand or a group of two people. The vision a leader casts sets the current and future direction of the organization. A shared vision ensures inclusivity for all to join in and participate. A shared vision directs everyone towards a common goal. The vision must have a forward-looking statement that is all-inclusive and projects a future not tied to any individual or group. Microsoft's vision demonstrated this in "To empower everyone on the planet to achieve more." How can a leader's vision be all-inclusive, build momentum, and continue for the future? Remember, the shared vision a leader casts as a leader must be more significant than any one individual. As a leader, spend time with individuals to understand their current realities and what they believe the future should be. Embedding their current reality with a shared vision of the future will drive towards positive outcomes for all. Continue to engage your organization with the vision through regular cadence meetings, ensuring the vision is purposely discussed at the beginning of each session, strengthening it within the current staff, providing newcomers become familiarized early on.

While frequent vision meetings should be held, consider bringing in outside sources for guidance and input. Engage a professional consulting organization that helps organizations with building and revising vision statements. An objective opinion often yields significant and undiscovered issues and provides potential solutions to common vision creation and implementation problems. Triune Leadership Services offers vision meetings at offsite locations. They hold workshops and one on one coaching with leaders and their organizations.[106] If contracting a professional organization is not possible right now, consider creating a local board from leaders with peer organizations familiar with the organization you lead with a genuine interest in its future. In return, agree to be part of their executive leadership board.

---

[106] (Deterding 2016).

CHAPTER 5

Designing and Building a High-Performance Culture through Servant Leadership

A servant leader should work to see the potential in their followers they interact with daily What traits, skillsets, qualities, and characteristics do they possess, and which ones should they grow and strengthen? What ingredients enable followers to become a great high-performing employees and receive fulfillment and satisfaction in their work? Similarly, what are the requirements to build a high-performing culture and organization that is vibrant, relevant, and resilient, especially in times of crisis or unforeseen circumstances? What should leaders include in their readiness and preparation to build a high-performing culture and organization? An organization with a high-performing culture will achieve financial and nonfinancial results that outperform its peers over time. Typically, these stellar results show up in quarterly or yearly financial statements, employee satisfaction surveys, and employee retention. This section will provide several critical elements for servant leaders to consider concerning culture and organizational design. While not inclusive, these elements will serve as a foundational base for an organization's early development, growth, and culture. It will also will provide insights, modern-day examples, and practical application for servant leaders to understand how to build a robust modern-day culture and high-performing organization.

The first step for today's leader is to hire the right people to support the organization. This has often been called or phrased as "getting the right people on the bus." The right people comprise of those followers who possess similar values, purpose, and mission that a leader holds and advocates daily. Values have already been already discussed in depth during chapter 4; however, values are critical not only during the performance of an organization but at the initial hiring process of each individual who makes up the organization. For example, Carroll Moon, CEO of Cloudfit Software states, "When we hire engineers, we are not necessarily looking for technical competency as the primary required trait; we look for a servant's heart attitude. We can always teach them technology." When selecting candidates for hire, what values do they aspire that aligns with your values as a leader? Do they value servant leadership characteristics or constructs of trust, humility, altruism, service, and love of people? Having the right values alignment early on will ensure the organization has cohesiveness and a forward-looking "one organization" approach.

Second, a leader should set expectations for the team and model the behavior for what success looks like. Not everyone will quickly align to the vision, mission, and purpose of the organization. A leader's task is to invest in their people to ensure they grow as followers and become leaders within themselves who will demonstrate and live out similar behaviors and actions. How can a servant-leader model the way for others? The first step, according to Deterding is to "surround yourself with high performers and with people who want to grow and who will challenge you."[107] While leaders need to understand their business in both depth and breadth of the organization, they cannot be expected to know everything that is known in each follower's mind. Here is where the value of trust and a trusting culture emerges. The leader trusts that those he leads will be respectful and honorable to carry out the tasks and demonstrate the appropriate behaviors in their relationship with the leader and others. To

---

[107] Deterding, 84.

strengthen and affirm a leader's knowledge and competencies, it is critical for a leader to surround themselves with high performers who will challenge them and stretch and help them grow. Some leaders also engage high professional coaches, while others seek similar development through professional organizations and peer leader groups. Creating a growth environment is critical for the success of the organization. This all begins with the leader modeling the way for themselves and those they interact with.

Third, a leader must also set expectations for the organization early on and hold each follower accountable to meet those expectations. While a servant leader may employ empowerment as a key cultural value, there is still the need for clarity in role and boundaries for what is expected over some time with measurement of performance. The leader employs conceptualization and foresight, key servant leader characteristics in an always forward-looking posture towards the future and planning early on. Given today's ever-dynamic and volatile, and uncertain political, social, and economic climate, both the leader and the followers they serve must remain agile and ready to pivot quickly. While an organization may have success early on, it cannot rely on this for future performance. The saying "history repeats itself" may be true in some cases but does not guarantee this will happen to a leader and their organization. To maintain consistently performing organization and sustaining momentum, the leader must ask, what can be done better or differently? What have we learned that has helped us grow as individuals and as a high-performing organization?

Third, having the right motives and attitudes is not enough for a high-performing organization. Every organization requires a process to follow for success. Having the proper process and performance measurements that match your organization and its high-performing momentum is critical. A leader should set the right expectations early on. Also, a leader should not set expectations that are well below the individual and organization's ability to attain. Set expectations that will cause some discomfort and stretch people beyond their expectations. For example, Elevation Church touts its bold and audacious goal of one hundred thousand in attendance for weekend

Worship Experiences. While at the time of this writing, they average over twenty-five thousand (multiple Worship Experiences) for a typical weekend, their consistent and purposeful expectations are well known. They stretch both the staff and volunteers to be persistent in inviting people from the surrounding communities every week. To Elevation's credit, investing early in online and TV media (Facebook, Twitter, YouTube, TBN) several years ago has added several thousand attendees through online experiences, which will likely continue to grow in tandem with in-person attendance.

Last, what agreed-on metrics or changes can be used to measure the success of the culture and organization? What key elements come to mind? While there are many other cultural values and characteristics that also contribute to an organization's cultural success, goodness or "God's goodness," stand out as on of the more important values. First, do both the leaders and the followers who serve each other look forward to their work most days? Do they value each other and seek good and success for each other? According to Borcarnea et al., goodness is "acting to benefit others."[108] Danker further strengthens this definition stating, "a positive moral quality characterized by interest and welfare of others.[109] Goodness leads to an overflowing of generosity, which in turn, becomes service to others. While there are many other cultural values and characteritics that also contribute to an organization's cultural success, goodness or "God's goodness," stands out as one of the more important values. Are leaders and followers seeking the good of others? Goodness will emerge in acts of kindness and sacrificial service to others. Yet the organization must still have quantifiable metrics aligned to goals demonstrating success or areas of improvement. Through the use of the acronym *SMART*, the following attributes will help with goal definement and achieve success. Research has shown SMART to be one of the most popular and proven methods.

---

[108] Borcarnea, Henson, Huizing, Mahan, and Winston, 87.
[109] Danker, 4.

Figure 1
SMART

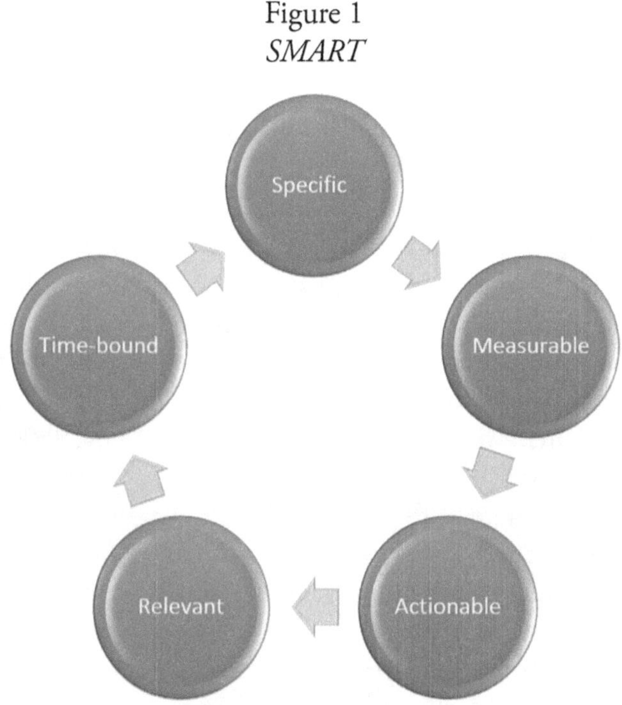

SMART helps both the leader and the organization follow a process to set specific and measurable goals. However, according to Reeves and Fuller, "SMART goals can be problematic."[110] In stable and very predictable organizations, there is a degree of certainty and expected probability. For example, Reeves and Fuller posit that industries such as "confectionary and cosmetics, grow with gross domestic product and follow relatively predictable trends."[111] To avoid these problematic results, they recommend identifying a specific destination or completing a goal and the time expected to reach that destination. This approach drives the right behaviors and actions to goal attainment. This process to measure and quantify results and outcomes is critical for leadership success and the organization.

---

[110] Reeves and Fuller, 1.
[111] Reeves and Fuller, 1.

Finally, having a robust and resilient strategy is key for any organization to maintain its culture and high organizational performance. "The focus of strategic leadership is the enduring performance potential of the organization—achieving the potential of the organization over time so that it will thrive in the long term."[112] Why is this important for leaders? Leaders and followers must have a solid understanding of the value they bring to the organization and contribute to the greater good and final results or outcomes. Leadership must recognize changes in the marketplace and adjust or completely change its strategy for relevance and competitiveness in order not only to survive but to thrive. For example, International Business Machines (IBM) was steadily declining in the late 1980s through 1993. However, the newly hired CEO, Lou Gerstner, changed the company's strategy from a "product-driven approach to a service-driven approach."[113] At the time of his appointment in 1993, IBM was about to be split into several smaller companies, which would significantly impact the employee base who many were long-time veterans with several years of service to the organization. The proposed changes in the culture and organization were bold and expedient.

Changes to HR policies, employee benefits, how they would function and work pivoted IBM from an old stagnate organization to a leading IT Service provider, once again admired and valued by all in the global marketplace. Did the culture and the expectations of leaders and those they served to change? Absolutely. What was vital for IBM's success was the willingness to change for the better of the organization and adopt a strategy that would bring them back into the arena as a top contributor and player in the Information Technology industry. According to Ackermann and Eden, "Gaining and sustaining competitive advantage is a natural focus of all for-profit organizations."[114] CEO Gerstner focused on keeping the company together by changing its values and organizational strategy to

---

[112] Hughes, Beatty, and Dinwoodie, 11.
[113] Hughes, Beatty, and Dinwoodie, 12.
[114] Ackermann and Eden, 1770.

rebuild and reinvigorate the organization as a critical contender in the global marketplace. While competitive advantage applies to for-profit organizations, this approach may also be used for nonprofits, especially those who espouse servant leadership, to identify the purpose and value they bring to their customers and stakeholders.

Examples of High-Performance Organizations and their Cultures in the Workplace

The following section will provide several examples of high-performing organizations and their cultures. These examples practice servant leadership characteristics and evident in their organizational culture.

Blackbaud

"At Blackbaud, our vision is to power an Ecosystem of Good® that builds a better world" (https://www.blackbaud.com/company/build-a-better-world).

Blackbaud (BLKB), founded in New York City, New York (1981), is a leading cloud computing provider that concentrates on serving the social good of philanthropic nonprofits, foundations, corporations, educational institutions, and religious organizations. The organizations they typically serve are the Central Texas Food Bank, Austin Humane Society, and Lady Bird Johnson Wildflower Center."[115] Their primary product focus is fundraising, relationship management, education administration, website management, and business analytics. The Blackbaud website states the organization seeks a better world, "One where everyone has meaningful opportunities to drive impact. One where we achieve more together than we can apart. One where good can take over." The culture and organizational performance are all built around service to others in the local community. For example, they offer their teams time off to volunteer

---

[115] (Rekdal 2018).

as a group at community service projects. Blackbaud believes every employee should be fully engaged in their lives outside of their work, ensuring a proper balance between the two. Their passion is helping nonprofits grow and thrive. Blackbaud's culture of one mission to serve others, especially nonprofits, brings the organization together and aligns towards the same goal. Blackbaud's passion for giving back is front in center for what they do and their purpose as a growing organization with purposeful intent on making the world a better place. By giving back a part of their culture, they contribute as individuals to an organization that serves a greater purpose to improve the world for all. All leaders and employees of Blackbaud all agree on the meaning of giving back, especially for nonprofits, which align with servant leadership characteristic of building community for the greater good of all. They also emphasize an always learning culture. Even their tenured sales executives with over fifteen years of service are still learning because of the various nonprofits they serve daily.

The key to their organizational success is remaining agile and making changes, such as the recent move of their on-premise software to the cloud. Brandon Phipps, VP of Sales and Market Development, says, "That transition, which is now largely complete, required us to reinvent all or internal processes without interrupting our clients' work. We had to be quick and adept at navigating changes."[116] Blackbaud is a unique philanthropic organization in that it merges social good and technology in its global pursuit for a better world. This is the catalyst that inspires each employee who desires to remain innovative with being part of the latest technology trends and also see how this impacts the lives and well-being of all. Through inclusivity and becoming more diverse, they can expand their touch and reach while growing their global social good footprint. Here again, the virtuous construct of Agapeo love, a very moral and respectful treatment of others aligns with their global social good pursuit. Blackbaud commits to an active culture of inclusivity by holding at least one event per month that all can participate in, such

---

[116] (Rekdal 2018).

as Pinewood Derby races, movie marathons, and progressive potluck dinners, are just a few examples. These cultural events with their full resource commitment to the growth of charities and remaining innovative powers the culture of the high-performing Blackbaud organization. Blackbaud has built its strategy around three key initiatives found on the Blackbaud website:

1. Unleash The Power of Data—Sharing data through their Blackbaud Institute for Philanthropic Impact provides insights and best practices to help guide a nonprofit strategy.
2. Drive Radical Collaboration—As a sustainable development goal, they Integrate what Blackbaud calls Global Goals taxonomy in its software for social good. This approach provides outcome mapping of their organization outcomes against a shared roadmap to ascertain progress compared to the global initiative.
3. Catalyze Individual Impact—Blackbaud listens to their employees to help define and drive their priorities, aligning with the servant leadership characteristic of listening. This also amplifies each employee's passion for serving others for the greater good of all as change agents with high impact.

Their commitment to building a better world is central to all of Blackbaud's activities and purpose as an organization.

CB Insights

"Five Cultural Traits: Hard Work, High Standards, Hunger, Helpfulness, Humility" (https://www.cbinsights.com/research-CBI-company-culture).

CB Insights, was founded in 2008 in New York City, New York, by Jonathan Sherry and Anand Sanwal, is a private company that provides market intelligence insights on private organizations and their investor relations. Their primary focus is on private equity, investment banking, and venture capital, providing key insights about growth organizations. They use machine learning for data analytics to gain information on industry trends that will lead to key business decisions from the knowledge gained. In this environment, all leaders and followers must remain agile and innovative in their technology adoption and use. Senior Marketing Manager Alyssa Anchelowitz says, "CB Insights focuses on employee growth and learning,"[117] which is key to remaining an active, forward-moving, and vibrant organization in the business analytics industry. The always learning approach and desire for more knowledge make the culture at CB Insights so attractive to current and prospective employees. They also prioritize individual development, a key characteristic of servant leadership and transformational leadership.[118] They wholly support the unique passion of each employee as this contributes to everyone becoming more engaged to work and grow as individuals to achieve what Greenleaf calls a "state of being."[119] CB Insights seeks employees who align their values to their five "H" traits: (1) hard work, (2) high standards, (3) hunger, (4) helpfulness, and (5) humility. They firmly believe open communications, humbleness, humility, and a willingness to help each other spurs employee innovation and growth, contributing to CB Insights' success. Here again, one can see the virtuous constructs of humility and service to others aligning with CB Insights' cultural and organizational values. Their website provides additional details on the five Hs:

1. Hard Work—Hard work focuses on solutions to a problem and the execution of the plan.
2. High Standards—High standards drive excellence in service and subject matter expertise attainment.

---

[117] (Rekdal 2018).
[118] (Cooper 2005).
[119] Greenleaf.

3. Hunger—Setting audacious goals and remain ever vigilant in pursuit of those goals.
4. Helpfulness—Providing clarity in communication and a commitment to follow through on your word with a willingness to adapt as needed.
5. Humility—Remaining open to others' opinions and position, giving them the opportunity to share their thoughts, emotions, and feelings respectfully.

CB Insights focuses on individual growth and achievement yet keeps its culture of always learning and adapting at the forefront of its organization's cultural traits and expectations.

Insights on Examples

Through the examples of Blackbaud and CB Insights, several cultural and organizational insights can be identified. First, the leader must always have the best interest of their followers front and center for continual innovation and growth of everyone. There should be an inclusive overall cultural value of giving back or seeking the good for all people through listening, investing in others' growth, humility, altruism, service, and building community. However, it is not enough to achieve positive results or outcomes. This approach requires continual examination of the culture to withstand unexpected or catastrophic events, ensuring the needs of individuals are aligned with the culture and have a forward-looking momentum for the organization. This approach will enable the organization to stay relevant and valuable to the people who serve the organization, its customers, and all other stakeholders.

An interview with Carroll M. Moon, Chief Technology Officer (CTO) of Cloudfit Software Inc.

Caroll Moon has twenty-five-plus years in the IT industry in various leadership roles developing and leading technical teams. In his current position, Carroll is responsible for solving CloudOps and DevOps scenarios for the IT industry leading Product Groups providing customer IT Solutions. Cloudfit software offers technology services to help customers run their IT Infrastructure effectively in the Cloud.

As a servant leader, what do you think your role is in building a high-performance culture and organization is? People write books on culture. People pontificate on culture. Culture is just about how people function as a team. The only way that I know to do it is the following:

1. To be very intentional to hire people with servant hearts who want to serve customers and teammates—to hire folks who don't "step on heads to get ahead."
2. To be very intentional about living the values that we want the team to model. People sniff out phonies very quickly. If the leaders aren't living it, we are wasting our time.
3. To be very intentional about positive reinforcement when we see the intended behavior and quickly and directly address any behavior counter to the intended behavior.
4. To recognize that every team is not for everyone. Sometimes, it is best for both parties if an individual who doesn't like the intended culture moves on to a team that is a better fit.

If given the opportunity, how would you go about building a high-performing organization and culture? What type of expectations and performance goals would you set? (Mr. Moon provided his responses based on what is documented on their website to this question https://www.cloudfitsoftware.com/cloudfit-vision-mission-core-values/). We still get asked about our unique value proposition. We have been delighted to participate in online interviews, podcasts, and magazine articles. We are thankful for the awards that we have won. And we are very grateful that other scale cloud providers and managed services providers call us to formalize partnerships. Still, what differentiates us is that our culture is to *serve*.

Our vision is to empower every business on the planet to transform at maximum velocity successfully. So many companies do not know where to start. We have the experts to help them cut through the noise to land on a plan. Other companies do not know how to move their business forward. We help. Other companies struggle with building the modern, [sometimes] cloud-born applications that will propel their business forward. We make those apps. Some companies have their apps figured out, but they struggle with having someone take accountability for the end-to-end outcomes of the application, including the "last mile," so we do that.

To achieve our vision to empower every business on the planet, we must scale. Thankfully, we built and ran some of the world's largest cloud infrastructures, so we can. Soon, our customers will start to see us bring our scenario capabilities to a pure SaaS model one by one. SaaS is Software as a Service Cloud solution as compared to Infrastructure as a Services (Iaas) and Platform as a Service (Paas). We will never stop. As we progress a scenario from consulting to software+humans to pure SaaS, we will iterate. And once a particular scenario reaches the SaaS delivery channel, we will continue to evolve that scenario forever. We will always provide more value on day N than we do on day 1. No exceptions. Our mission is to modernize our client's complete IT portfolio through technology and human accountability. One of our core values is extreme accountability. We will take accountability for the entire portfolio by taking accountability for all of the applications in the portfolio one by one. Or, we will take accountability for a piece of one application that is a tiny fraction of the portfolio. For example, we are happy to take accountability for the entire new ERP platform (including writing the platform). We are pleased just to take accountability for the end-to-end monitoring outcomes. We always try to meet the exact customer need to fill any gaps rather than sell a square peg for a round hole. Our people, our approach, and our platform all allow that flexibility. In the end, we are accountable.

Even before accountability, though, our culture is to *serve*. Our values are the following:

1. *Servant leadership.* We are here to serve our customers. We are not here to sell. If we can provide value, we will. If we cannot, we will recommend another partner.

2. *Extreme accountability.* We do what we say we will do—no matter what.

3. *Results-driven.* The only thing that matters to your business is the outcome, so the only thing that matters to us is the outcome. We often say, "we do not sell software; we sell outcomes."

4. *Velocity.* If business outcomes are the only things that matter, then the speed of achieving those outcomes is a critical focus for every customer. CloudFit Software is so focused on helping our customers achieve velocity; our software platform has the internal codename "Velocity"; it is publicly known as "CloudFit Software" or "CFS."

5. *Empowerment.* Our entire existence is about enabling our customers. We are happy to do it all for them, we are so glad to just plug gaps for them, and we are pleased to just teach/consult/coach them on how to do it themselves. We meet our customers where they are to empower them to be successful.

In the spirit of our goal to *serve*, we thought it would be an excellent step to tell the world publicly what we stand for. We know that imitators will enter the industry—they are already showing up. Imitation is flattering, and we welcome it. We even accept it when these tremendous partners approach us to white-label our services under them to help their customers. There is an infinite number of customer+application combinations today and tomorrow, and we aim to serve them all. So come one, come all. We are here to help.

How would you measure individual and organizational performance and behaviors? The answers I provided to the first question address this question. Also, it's a big part of every meeting. Every all-hands meetings. Every performance review. Everything we do is wrapped around those values and *serve.*

How would you evaluate and measure your effectiveness as a servant leader? I seek feedback from God. I seek God's answers for decisions. Not everyone at CloudFit believes what I believe, and that's ok. But I believe what I believe, and I seek answers from Whom I seek answers.

I am also very self-critical. I constantly evaluate my actions, words, facial expressions, etc., during meetings, after meetings, during conversations, etc. I do not try to fake anything; instead, my goal is to be authentic. I want to be 100 percent real. But I also want to be kind. Being authentic doesn't give me an excuse to be rude. I can be blunt but with love. I also seek feedback from my inner circle. We are honest with one another. I am real with them, and I ask them to be honest with me.

Practical Application

Developing, building, and sustaining a high-performing culture and organization requires commitment and hard work. It takes considerable effort for an organization to emerge as a dynamic and growing organization; it is just as much effort, if not more, to maintain that momentum once the organization has been established. The following steps provided below will guide leaders and their followers to begin forming a high-performing culture and organization. These steps have been gathered from academic scholarly research and popular press publications. While not inclusive, they will quickly develop and strengthen an organization's culture and set it on a path toward high performance.

Leadership: leaders and followers

In most modern-day organizations, effective and successful leadership is a scarce source. Leaders cannot rely on the old command and control approach from sixty years or seventy years ago to motivating followers. To be effective, leaders must think strategically, set expectations, create momentum, develop and build employee engagement, hold people accountable, including themselves, deliver quality and quantifiable results in a short time. One of the keys to building high-performing teams is providing clear direction and creating a sense of urgency towards a goal or purpose. For effectiveness, a leader must develop and sustain long-term relationships with their followers. This is achieved by investing in the follower for their success by understanding their needs and desires, developing a career path that challenges and fulfills their inner passions, and finally, helps them transform and grow as servant leaders. An effective leader casts a vision motivating followers to align and espouse that same vision with purpose, intent, and passion for achieving the expected outcomes. As a leader, clarify and continually resound the organization's purpose, values, and mission to the organization. A leader also provides clarity for expectations of both the team and the individual. Finally, they ensure the strategy, what they are trying to accomplish as a team, is clearly understood.

People as a strategic asset

The most important core asset of every organization are the employees who agree to contribute to the success of the mission and vision of that organization. High-performing organizations communicate and translate their business strategy into an exciting and vibrant people strategy, thus attracting and retaining high-caliber talent. These types of organizations have a well-thought-out "Strategic Human Resource Development (SHRD)" process or methodology.[120] Here human resources (HR) plays a crucial role in advising and guiding the organization's business units or groups for operational and people development. A strong SHRD will provide "a clear vision about people's abilities and potential and operates within the overall strategic framework of the business"[121] Organizations should design, align, and integrate SHRD into their lines of business for a high-performing culture and organization. For example, by investing in training and giving employees exposure and experience to other business sectors, they will grow as individuals and leaders. SHRD plays a critical role in this process.

---

[120] Carbery and Cross, 31.
[121] Carbery and Cross, 31.

Organizational design

When designing a high-performing culture and organization, much consideration must be given to the organizational structure or chain of command and how communication is designed. Leaders should be clear on what matters most to the people who serve them. The structure should be forward-looking and thinking, yet with flexibility to pivot quickly, if needed. According to Burton et al., "Organizational design is an ongoing executive process that includes both short-term, routine changes, as well as intermittent, larger-scale changes."[122] For example, organizations that are lean in structure enable them to enact change quickly and efficiently, helping leaders and followers to stay focused on meaningful work. This drives value, resiliency, and longevity to the organization. While this may not be possible for larger corporations to enact a lean structure such as International Business Machines (IBM), Microsoft (MSFT), or General Motors (GM), given their global footprint and size, always having a focus to reduce or minimize unneeded structural layers that hinder or slow the organization should be continually evaluated and adjusted accordingly.

Change management

In today's modern organizations, change is a dynamic and continual phenomenon. Leaders and the organizations they serve to achieve success and sustain competitive advantage over their competition must remain agile to political, social, and economic changes in the marketplace. Second, they must have a consistent approach or process to implement and drive change for their business strategy, structure, focus, and organizational culture. "Strategies inherently require a change from the organization and the people within it."[123] Leaders need to ensure their organization is continually learning new

---

[122] Burton, Obel, and Hakonsson, 10.
[123] Hughes, Beatty, and Dinwoodie, 47.

skills, advancing in knowledge growth and capabilities, and agile enough to pivot when a change is required. A leader must also be aware of the emotional challenges that face organizations for those who may resist or not change as expected. Having empathy as a leader for those they lead and serve will support and help with organizational changes.

While change is necessary for all organizations, maintaining a continual feedback loop or listening system is critical. Leaders must understand what the change has done from a performance implication and the human emotional element of the follower. This is where servant leadership characteristics of listening, empathy, awareness, persuasion, foresight, and building community should be employed. These characteristics enable leaders to adjust and continually evaluate how successful the change is and what the required next steps may be. Clarity and setting expectations are top of mind for the leader during transition. A leader should clarify their accountablities and the follower's accountabilities for implementing and tracking the change. Communication from the top down and back up to the top of the organization is imperative for successful changes in the organization.

Culture development and engagement

While culture has been defined and discussed in earlier chapters, cultural development and engagement build upon employee engagement because their work brings meaning to them personally and professionally. The culture of an organization, how work is accomplished is shaped to achieve strategic goals. Through engagement and strategic intent, employees are motivated to go beyond the call of duty in pursuit of those corporate objectives. Having a dynamic and vibrant culture will accelerate the organization's strategic goals. Leaders must continually monitor, evaluate, and manage their culture to succeed in their strategy when the process changes, so too should the culture in tandem. A high-performing organization will keep a tight pulse on the culture for employee engagement and measure goal attainment success. Often, culture is tested for its strength during difficult times where fragile relationships are exposed. The task for leaders is to ensure employee engagement reflects the organization's culture where employees feel and live out their personal and professional aspirations in pursuit of the organization's strategic goals.

Creating Trust and Long-Lasting Relationships

Trust must be present in all organizations for both leaders and followers to form a cohesive relationship to achieve specific outcomes or objectives. Over the last thirty years, scholarly academic and popular press publications have increasingly focused on the topic of trust, most notably, in servant leadership academic and popular press articles. A culture of trust produces higher individual and organizational performance engagement, increased morale, and improved bottom line profits. According to Harvard research Professor Paul J. Zak, "Compared with people at low-trust companies, people at high-trust companies report 74% less stress, 106% more energy at work, 50% higher productivity, 13% fewer sick days, 76% more engagement, 29% more satisfaction with their lives, and 40% less burnout."[124] Trust creates and promotes joy when employees feel a sense of higher purpose in their work. Trust and joy work in tandem, producing positive results for leadership and the organization. Trust is a crucial servant leadership characteristic that requires development and sustainability throughout the relationship of two or more people agreeing to engage and collaborate, no matter the topic or task at hand.

---

[124] (Zak 2017).

This section will provide several thoughts and insights for servant leaders to contemplate regarding creating trust and long-lasting relationships. While not inclusive, these points will provide a foundational basis for understanding and comprehending what trust is and how it is formed in organizations. The following narrative will provide insights, modern-day examples, and practical application for servant leaders to gain an understanding of how to create, develop, and sustain long-lasting relationships to withstand unexpected change and uncertainty in turbulent times.

Followers and the organization they serve seek leaders they can build confidence in or faith that they will follow through in both their words and actions, especially under complex, uncertain, and stressful times. In tandem, leaders must also have confidence in their followers in a similar or reciprocal relationship. Without both having this type of relationship, nothing of significance will be accomplished or achieved. A leader may perform some tasks or accomplishments through fear or compliance because of dutiful expectations, but this is short-term, and often leads to followers leaving the organization's role. A lack of trust diminishes influence and erodes the culture of the organization. Effective leaders of high moral character are purposeful and intentional in their pursuit to build and foster trust throughout the organization.

Conversely, Joseph and Winston state, "Trust is the level confidence that one individual has in another's competence and his or her willingness to act in a fair, ethical, and predictable manner."[125] The behavior of the leader begins the process of trust with followers. Trust will either grow or decline based on how vulnerable the leader is and allow their vulnerabilities to become exposed to their followers. For example, does the leader readily admit error on his or her part? Do they demonstrate humility in accepting responsibility and accountability for their actions, especially when they were incorrect or failed in their assumptions?

---

[125] Joseph and Winston, 6–7.

When there is little or no trust in an organization, fear becomes prevalent, and everyone goes into a self-protection or preservation mode. This type of behavior will cause unnecessary, unproductive energy to protect themselves instead of performing with excellence. Open communication for both the leader and the follower is paramount if trust is to emerge as a leading characteristic of the organization and a healthy, vibrate culture. For example, Microsoft Corporation states, "We run on trust" (https://www.microsoft.com). They make clear that if something's not right and a customer reports an issue, they can expect the issue to be addressed in the utmost expedient, serious, and fair manner. Most people value consistency and predictability from their leaders, especially during a crisis or uncertain times. Leaders who have a routine in their daily work rhythm create consistency and predictability for their followers to engage and model similar behaviors. Leaders demonstrate these behaviors through routine meetings, setting clear and understandable expectations, and taking the time to invest in their follower's wants, needs, and desires. This relationship does not happen automatically. It requires many transactional engagements that lead to more in-depth conversations, growing, and building a solid, sustainable relationship. Ultimately, the relationship becomes so strong that the question of trust between the leader and follower is no longer part of the discussion; it is automatically inferred because the focus is on the success of the follower and the organization.

Trust should be a significant part of the organizational culture. An organizations culture is shaped through

- what they pay attention to and reward;
- the way they allocate resources;
- role modeling;
- how they deal with critical incidents; and
- the criteria they use for recruitment, selection, promotion, and dismissal.[126]

---

[126] Joseph and Winston, 8.

These characteristics of trust shape the relationship between the leader's behavior and how the follower reacts and responds to them. Credibility will begin to emerge, and followers will perceive their leader as trusting individuals and organizational leaders. In tandem, servant leadership emphasizes the good and well-being of the follower over the leader's self-interest, promoting the development of the follower for their benefit and future.

Creating and sustaining trust in any organization is no easy or quick task for servant leaders who often do not interface daily with the people they lead and serve. Trust is critical for all relationships, especially when there is a lack of information and understanding. So what is trust in its simplistic form? Trust believes in another group or individual whom a leader becomes vulnerable within, sharing valuable information or confidence they will meet expectations. A leader takes faith in their followers not to harm or purposely use it to the leader's detriment. Trust often comes in three specific forms: "contractual trust, competence trust, and communication trust." See Figure 1. Contractual trust is based upon the character and belief or faith that someone will do what is expected based upon the agreed boundaries between the two parties. Competence trust arises when there is mutual respect of knowledge and skill set of individuals or groups. Because of their competence, the trusting individual will give benefit of doubt to the knowledgeable resource and agree to decisions or outcomes. Communication trust builds upon the open sharing of information, disclosing mistakes, and making one vulnerable.

A Strategic Leadership Team (SLT) must practice and implement behavior characteristics of these three forms for the organization to grow and develop a cultural climate of trust, which will lead to a healthy, vibrant, and dynamic organizational culture that can withstand unexpected changes crises. An environment of trust must form and always be exercised. SLTs should build in their design how trust can be incorporated and kept alive for the organization to achieve its strategic goals and objects. Trust is a critical measurement for a healthy organizational climate for how the internal organization functions and operates. SLTs are responsible for ensuring trust is included in organizational design and achieving strategic goals. Trust builds teamwork and strategic alliances both within the internal and the external environment. The following figure below shows how these three forms work together in building organizational trust.

Figure 1
Forms of Trust

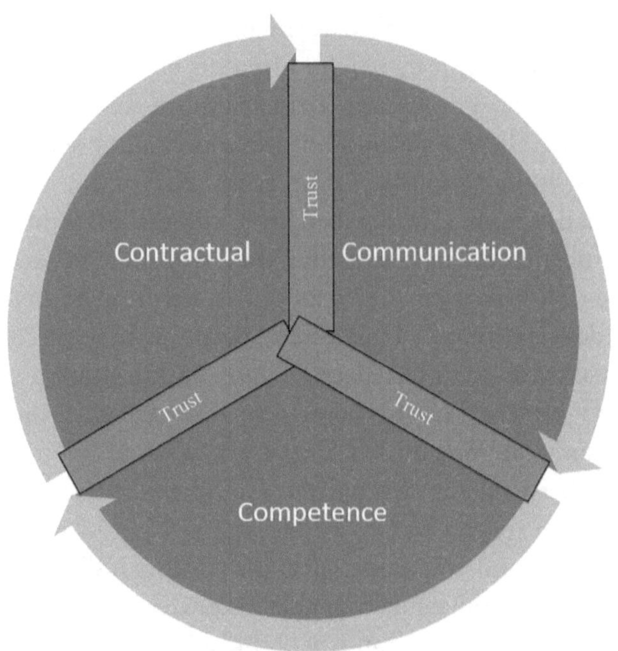

According to Sendjaya, a covenantal relationship is developed through "mutual commitment by individuals characterized by shared values, open-ended commitment, mutual trust, and concern for the welfare of others."[127] Here followers see and feel their value from leaders, creating a unique synergy that results in both positive individual and organizational outcomes. Over time, followers become highly trustworthy, loyal, engaging, and willing to go above and beyond what is expected because they always desire to serve. A leader can

---

[127] Sendjaya, 71.

only build mutual trust in others by showing vulnerability, freely sharing information, and supporting their followers, even in times of failure. A leader will accept their followers for who they are and respect them like people, no matter their title or position. A leader's values will become shared when the follower genuinely cares for them and is willing to take risks, even if there is a high probability of failure.

McNulty states, "Trust is at the foundation of cooperative and collaborative leadership."[128] However, Patterson posit trust is "about being linked to integrity, respect for others, and service to the organization."[129] Trust is paramount in an organization for weathering a global event. How is trust formed? A leader must be vulnerable, open to perspectives and ideas, and employ two-way communications with those the leader engages with. Trust is earned over multiple conversations, actions, and behaviors. How does a leader know trust is established? When they see their leader emulating and living out the virtues of a servant leader discussed earlier.

Examples of Leaders and Organizations Who are Considered Trustworthy

This section will highlight examples of leaders known as trustworthy leaders in business investing and the United States Military.

Warren Buffett (Berkshire Hathaway, CEO)

"Trust is like the air we breathe—when it's present, nobody really notices; when it's absent, everybody notices" (https://quotefancy.com/warren-buffett-quotes).

Warren Edward Buffett, born August 30, 1930, is currently chairman and CEO of Berkshire Hathaway. Mr. Buffett is also an American investor and global business tycoon, with a net worth of

---

[128] McNulty, 2.
[129] Patterson, 5.

over $100 billion as of April 2021. Much of his business success came from "arbitrage techniques, short-term trading, liquidations, and so on."[130] Mr. Buffett is known for his value investing approach and living a straightforward and frugal life, despite his accumulated wealth over the years. Mr. Buffett is also known as a significant philanthropist who will give away 99 percent of his wealth at the time of death. He also co-founded The Giving Pledge with other billionaires such as Bill Gates, pledging to give away at least half of their wealth to philanthropic causes (https://givingpledge.org). While he may not be portrayed as a servant leader as compared to others discussed earlier, his values and beliefs align with several servant leadership virtuous constructs of altruism, humility, and love of people. However, trust, another virtuous construct, is ever-present in his life and admired by many people across the globe.

Mr. Buffett believes trust is paramount for any organization to succeed. For example, in his company Berkshire Hathaway "The company takes a famously hands-off approach to management, delegating all responsibility to the heads of its subsidiaries. The trust-based approach works because the most important quality Berkshire looks for in a new manager and companies is trust—they pass up opportunities if they have a shred of doubt about trustworthiness."[131] Organizations that base their culture on trust promote autonomy and accountability. In this regard, trust can have a substantial influence on followers and can serve as a powerful motivator. At Berkshire Hathaway, trust is built upon autonomy, which develops accountability and responsibility in the follower and the leader.

According to Mr. Buffett, his role as leader of Berkshire Hathaway is to have a vision and goals for the organization and then have them accomplished through other people. Being a visionary is critical to predicting strategically where the company should pursue its efforts. He believes his role is to achieve the vision through other people. With over 150,000 people now working for Berkshire

---

[130] Altucher, 3.
[131] (Cunningham 2020).

Hathaway, multiple operating managers are CEOs of their own business, without any direction from the HQ office. According to Mr. Buffett, he gives leaders a feeling of ownership and freedom from autonomy to "paint the picture they choose every day" (Buffett 2020)(Buffett 2020). He likened his leadership style to a baseball game where his managers are given the opportunity to swing the bat every day to have impact. However, he sends a memo every two years (the only form of required communication) to each manager, with the following guidance that has not changed since the inception of Berkshire Hathaway. He states that they can afford to lose money, even a lot of money; however, they cannot afford to lose reputation. He wants to ensure that everything can be reported from all operating companies without issue in any publication. He goes on to say, "It took us 37 years to gain our reputation. However, we can lose this in 37 minutes."[132] Reputation is critical to Mr. Buffett in business. He is willing to sacrifice profits to ensure a spotless reputation. His authentic leaderships speaks volumes of his character as a leader, especially when communicating expectations for the future.

Robin Blanchard (Retired United States Military Colonel)

"Accomplished Leader and Speaker, Retired Military Colonel, Business Consultant, & Executive Coach" (https://www.robin-blanchard.com/about).

Robin Blanchard is a retired military colonel serving in the United States National Guard who has lived a life of service while in the military. Robin became the first female in the State of Washington National Guard to command a brigade. She has also has spoken on leadership to community leaders in other countries, university students, and military leaders. Outside of her military service, she has served the public as a health systems consultant for the Washington State Department of Health, including several board leader positions on nonprofit organizations within the state and local community. She

---

[132] (Buffett 2020).

is also an adjunct professor at George Washington University teaching leadership and has presented several keynote sessions on leadership. At present, she is a Consulting Partner for the Ken Blanchard Companies, where her expertise is in helping clients actively listen and build communication skills to grow and strengthen their performance in the workplace.

While serving in the military, Robin employed servant leadership characteristics in her leadership style and approach for building and sustaining trusting relationships with those she engaged with. She firmly believes it was a privilege and honor to serve as the first female brigade commander for the Washington National Guard.[133]She said the military did not always support her approach of servant leadership, putting others first. The military is very direct and expects obedient and immediate action upon command. Yet Robin understood that to have people respond quickly and complete tasks with excellence, "followership must be earned."[134] This is where trust is built, when a leader and follower engage in mutual respect and agreement to work together for the good of the organization and the individual's success, even at the cost of a leader's success or personal sacrifice. According to Robin, not only does a servant leader need to be technically competent, but they must also earn respect, honor, and trust from their followers. This is what she calls earning, "the hearts and minds of their troops. That takes a real servant leader."[135] Leadership is a heart issue. Here the goal of a servant leader is to win the heart of each follower, so much so that they will act upon request with total commitment, thereby becoming a servant leader in themselves for other people's good.

During her twenty-eight-year career in the military as an officer, she realized two critical elements of a servant leader when leading others: (1) People have a deep desire to be loved and valued, and (2) followers require an environment with the proper tools and resources to achieve success. Robin makes clear her focus is ensuring her fol-

---

[133] (Blanchard and Broadwell 2018).
[134] Blanchard and Broadwell, 189.
[135] Blanchard and Broadwell, 190.

lowers know they are valued through acknowledging them, always praising them, and empowering them at work. These few actions is what builds confidence and trust in followers when done consistently and purposefully. Praise ignites passion and momentum in followers, which leads to the success of the follower and the organization they serve.

In tandem, trust is critical to the success of all organizations. Trust flows from the top of an organization down to the bottom. Trust requires work to develop and just as much effort to maintain. According to Robin, "Soldiers feel valued when their leaders prove they will back them up."[136] She also states that "a person be motivated at work when they feel safe to use all of their abilities and take some risk…most innovation begins with someone taking a risk"[137] To Robin, her best approach to leadership is servant leadership, giving people purposefully, meaningful praise, empowering them, and keeping a focus on their success. This behavior approach and style leads to solid and resilient trusting relationships, especially during difficult or uncertain events. Her personal goal as a servant leader is "to care more about the success of others than your own."[138] Care for others leads to confidence and faith in them, which results in a trusting reciprocal relationship.

Insights on Examples

Trust can be a powerful tool to motivate followers in any organization. Conversely, the lack of trust can cause an organization to falter and ultimately fail in its goals and strategic objectives. Each of the examples above show how trust immerges in reputation of a leader and their desire for success of the follower. In tandem, autonomy gives the follower freedom to work within their thoughts and processes to complete a task or assignment with little oversight, including the flexibility to take risks and fail. Yet from failure, a

---

[136] Blanchard and Broadwell, 191.
[137] Blanchard and Broadwell, 191.
[138] Blanchard and Broadwell, 194.

leader and follower learn the most about becoming better people in serving their organizations. Trust in an organization produces effective leadership and followership, a vibrant and resilient culture, and a high-performing organization.

An interview with Hector Valenzuela, Customer Success account manager, Microsoft on Trust

Hector is a twenty-four-year servant leader that has direct experience in services, manufacturing, and people leadership. He has spent twenty-two years in power generation in various capacities, supply chain, product group marketing, and sales excellence. Hector has led multiple high-performance teams since 2006 in areas that include operations and sales. His understanding of clients is unique because he sees customer success through the lens of execution and commercial pursuit.

In your opinion and understanding, what is Trust, especially with individuals and the organizations they serve? Trust is the one element that comes with an intrinsic value. Trust must be earned and developed over time through multiple transactions and the leader's authenticity, manifesting through their action. It is one thing to provide the direction; the other is to live out the direction.

Earlier in my career, I recall a full bird (rank in military) colonel I reported to who looked to a senior leader in our organization for insights. He then came to me as the younger in the group. He told me, "I always look to experience, but with you, there is a counterbalance to experience with younger perspectives." I actually became empowered as a result of his investment in me as a leader. He began to talk to me at a much more mature level. From this, I learned to trust him immediately. Not only was he giving me direction, but he was also showing me the reasons why he had become successful himself. Everything he was doing was authentic and empowering the team, investing in the right people. Through empowerment, I earned his trust. This made me fire on all cylinders, elevating my performance for him. As a result, I received awards for my abilities, catapulting my career into leadership, managing teams since 2005. It takes five to ten years to get experience in leadership to where I could take on more significant leadership roles.

To build trust, what types of actions and behaviors should a leader employ to build trust with them and for organizational trust to thrive? First of all, every authentic leader that they lead with trust. This is something they should live through daily, feeling the sentiment and connect with this. If you inspire trust, this is the most significant connection for all you serve, both employees, customers, family, and society in general. How authentic do you present yourself in meetings? What would others say about you when you are not present? Trust is the absolute keystone in ensuring a connection, no matter who it is.

Second, the actual presence that you command. When you have a presence, it projects confidence, experience, well-roundedness. When you are actually in a moment in trying to communicate with people, you engage with them through trust and presence. You are manifesting trust through presence.

Third, absolute communication is tantamount. When you have absolute communication, you are building trust through simplified, concise, and clear communication. Whoever it is you are communicating with can make sense and embrace the logic of what you are saying. Being able to connect and say, "I am absolutely communicating," is critical.

What recommendations or advice would you give another leader to build trusting relationships in an organization? To build trust, you must be able to do this through the lens of servant leadership, immersing yourself in others who are feeling in the moment—being able to absorb what others are thinking about you and what you are trying to communicate. Trust comes from investing in others and them investing back in you. It is crucial to understand and know your audience. A message that is effective with one audience may not be compelling with another. You must be authentic in your message for the audience too feels connected with their personality.

If trust were ever broken or fractured, which often happens in organizations, how would you rebuild and heal this situation? You must put yourself in the situation and ask how my behavior has led to the moment. It must start with understanding and owning your behavior that has led to the broken or fractured trust. You must be able to face the fractured trust with courage and confidence to restore the relationship. This is about you being vulnerable to be able to say, "this is on me; let's start over." It's about bringing the issue back to the center and focus on whatever is creating that conflict.

Practical Application

Over the last fifty to sixty years, leaders across all organizations have tried various strategies and tactics to improve employee moral and engagement. Most often, this has led to short-term retention and low performance in organizations. However, creating and maintaining a culture of trust, leaders, and followers can turn these poor results around by providing clear direction, equipping their people for success through investing in their future, and empowering them to achieve great results with little supervision or oversight. Treating followers like adults, allowing them to take risks, and perform at their best will yield positive moral and financial results. The following six leader behavior and action recommendations will encourage and grow trust in all organizations that can be measured and guided to improve overall organization performance.

Acknowledge excellence in work

Excellence in work requires a commitment to positive behavior characteristics, even when someone is not monitored or watched. This means completing a task to the best of one's ability and desire for others to emulate in tandem. In turn, leaders should practice altruism in holding others above themselves so much, so they give all recognition and benefit to the follower. This act has an immense implication on building a trusting organization. Recognition of excellent work, especially in a public arena, forms a bond for both leaders and peer followers to move and grow positively. Some examples to start building trust would be quarterly awards that either achieved specific metrics or leader/peer-nominated. As discussed earlier, 3M used a point system that was inclusive no matter years of service or achievement; everyone was included in acknowledgment of excellence over time.

Intellectual stimulation

Intellectual stimulation involves the leader challenging and encouraging the follower to become innovative and creative in solving problems and dilemmas. Northouse states, "It encourages followers to think things out on their own and engage in careful problem-solving"[139] Here the leader keeps the work at the center of the followers' thoughts and motivates them to achieve the goal or task at hand. The leader guides the follower through the process as a coach or mentor through uncharted waters or scenarios. Leaders ask questions such as, what can be done differently, and how can we do things differently? Steven Jobs, the founder of Apple Inc., was known for this approach and lived out this transformational leadership characteristic every day at Apple. When followers see they are thinking innovatively and achieving progress toward a realistic goal, they feel a sense of accomplishment and find value and purpose in their work.

Create and foster empowerment

Empowerment is a virtuous construct of servant leadership. This characteristic focuses on enabling followers to perform at their best. According to Dierendonck and Patterson, empowerment "aims at fostering proactive, self-confident attitude among followers, and gives them a sense of personal power."[140] How should a leader employ empowerment? Here the leader gives the follower full autonomy for a project or task to be carried out with little guidance or oversight. However, in times of failure or struggle, the leader sees this as a learning opportunity and growth for their followers.

---

[139] Northouse, 192.
[140] Dierendonck and Patterson, 158.

Enable transparency and demonstrate vulnerability

As a leader, always remain open about the current state of the business and the direction the organization is heading, especially if turbulent and uncertain times are in the near future. The more transparent and open you are as a leader, the greater the trust from followers. Open communications are critical for the formation and maintenance of trust in the organization. Zak purports, "A 2015 study of 2.5 million manager-led teams in 195 countries found that workforce engagement improved when supervisors had some form of daily communication with direct reports."[141] Even in difficult times, when leaders are open to their followers about the current circumstances, trust can still survive if not thrive during this time. For example, holding weekly communications with strategic direction and vision can serve as to the lifeline between all leaders and followers in an organization. Leaders scheduling regular town hall meetings and individual one-on-one meetings with open and question and answer opportunities will also further strengthen trust in the organization. A leader who shows vulnerability and genuine service to others demonstrate their character of humility, further building upon trust. In addition, trust can be formed when a senior leader purposely delegates a task or project down to another Jr. leader or follower, growing follower competencies and strengths.

Cultivate and sustain lasting relationships

A leader must tirelessly build, cultivate, and sustain relationships with everyone they engage with, such as customers, peers, followers, and leadership. Trust is a 360 circular relationship. Here is where servant leaders invest in the follower, seeking what is best for them, so much so, they will sacrifice their recognition and financial success for the follower to receive the full benefit. This is true for the other stakeholders mentioned earlier. While traditional leadership

---

[141] (Zak 2017).

approaches focus on motivating followers to complete the assigned tasks, the servant leader focuses on the relationship first and then the work at hand. How does this form of trust show up at work? When a leader offers to help, others achieve a goal or objective without thought or concern for themselves. Selfless giving and serving all those they interact. Trust begins with small incremental transactional engagements, leading to more prominent forms of engagement and communication. How can you start with building a long-lasting relationship of trust? Spend time by investing in followers over lunch or after-hour get-togethers. Schedule regular team-building activities, either remote or in-person that are offsite from the everyday work environment. Ask those you interact with what is important to them when they are at work. Everyone has varied values and beliefs. Some may want career advancement, where others may wish to flexibility in schedule for personal reasons. This is the task of the leader to build and sustain a social-bonding environment in the workplace. When people genuinely care about each other, they will go outside of their comfort zone to help others in time of need and help them achieve quality of life.

Foster and encourage continual people development

Organizations with high trust have leaders who will invest in developing people professionally and personally. This approach helps the follower to achieve a state of being and grow in self-actualization. It is not enough to just acquire more knowledge or skills; every follower and leader must grow as a human being. Otherwise, performance will suffer. Leaders who have what CEO Satya Nadella of Microsoft calls, "A Growth Mindset,"[142] which seeks to develop followers to reach their full potential. By setting clear goals and expectations, allowing autonomy to achieve stated goals, and including consistent feedback will move the follower to improved performance and improve their ability to grow as a whole person. Leaders must

---

[142] Nadella.

focus on helping followers advance in the role, invest in the career development of their people, and ensure they are balancing work requirements with personal responsibilities outside of the workplace.

CHAPTER 7

Developing and Sustaining a
Servant Leader's Character

Over the last thirty years, leaders and the organizations they serve around the globe have faced unprecedented and surmounting political, social, and economic challenges. Most recently, COVID-19, a global pandemic, impacted every person across the globe in one form or another in their lives.[143] This pandemic brought forth and tested a leader's character for how they respond to sudden and unexpected events in their organization, changing their leadership approach and making decisions for their organization. During these times, a leader's character and behavior are tested for strength and validity for all to observe and respond to. Character is critical to excellence in leadership, especially to how followers and groups in the organization make decisions, engage with customers, hire new employees, honor and respect current employees, and what they want to be known for as an organization. This section will provide an in-depth discussion on what character is in a leader, how it is displayed, modern-day examples of leaders who are known for displaying stellar character traits, an interview with a modern-day leader on their thoughts for character development, and finally, specific exam-

---

[143] (Seijts and Milani 2019).

ples on how a leader, especially a servant leader, can develop and strengthen positive character traits for others to emulate.

Character is a key and relevant component of effective leadership that results from the behaviors and actions of a leader, especially a servant leader. Character, as defined by Wright, is "the pattern of thinking and acting which runs right through someone, so that wherever you cut into them (as it were), you see the same person through and through."[144] How a leader and their followers interact with the world around them in conversations and actions puts their character value and traits on display for all to see and experience. Also, how a leader construes feedback, what they chose to take immediate action upon, how they engage in conflict, setbacks, and failures shows their character. Character is a conscious effort to seek to demonstrate and live out the right behaviors, so much so that it becomes second nature, requiring no thought about what the right thing is to do in a situation or circumstance.

Character development is often formed through three specific actions or behaviors. First, a leader or follower must have a specific target or goal they are seeking to achieve, such as being more aware of others needs and helping meet them, attaining a financial goal of paying off debt, or purposely acknowledging or putting others first above oneself, similar to servant leader characteristics of humility and altruism. A leader should ask themself, what do I want to change or strengthen for positive behaviors or characteristics and commit to change? Second, develop a roadmap or plan to achieve stated goals or objectives with key milestones, including accountability towards the goal. An example would be a professional development plan showing progress for of career objectives that would incorporate servant leadership characteristics discussed earlier.

A second example would be to engage with other people, practicing empathy and listening—in other words, becoming more purposeful for being in the moment for others, especially during emotional and times of crisis. Finally, third repeat those steps or processes

---

[144] Wright, 27.

multiple times to where the desired change becomes habitual and second nature over time. As a leader, the behavioral change will emerge without thought or need to evaluate; doing the right thing at the right time. For the Christian, it is the Holy Spirit working in their lives daily, refining, chaffing, and renewing an individual's character, modeled the characteristics of love, joy, peace, patience, kindness, gentleness, goodness, faithfulness, and finally, self-control (Gal. 5:22–23 NIV).

A leader's disposition, not the position, is what determines their character. How does a leader respond in times of crisis or unexpected events that impact follower's emotions and state of being? Their attitude, perspective, and calm demeanor will bring forth their character attributes. It is imperative for leaders, especially servant leaders, to maintain what Seijts and Milani call "interconnectedness" with all people they interact with.[145] COVID-19 completely changed how leaders and the organizations they serve, engage in daily communications. With no large gatherings of people beyond six or more and maintaining a six-foot social distance while wearing a face mask, has completely changed everyone's ability to communicate nearby routinely. Interconnectedness seeks to "sense and value deep connections with others at all levels within the organizations, communities, and society—is an important part of the character dimension of collaboration."[146] Leaders must be purposeful in establishing and maintaining relationships early on with all those they engage with, especially during times of crisis. While a leader may have a title or be seen as a person of authority, their human approach of servant leadership, listening, caring, empathy, trust, love, and service will strengthen and reaffirm their character.

A high-character leader is also a consistent optimist and finds the good in all situations, despite the circumstances or dilemma. They seek to help others through service without acknowledgment or recognition. Leaders of character are often behind the scenes, complet-

---

[145] Seijts and Milani, 2.
[146] Seijts and Milani, 2.

ing tasks or projects that others may have abandoned or are unable to complete. Yet they pursue and keep the effort afloat as they see the value or the goodness in the work or the individual they are helping. Goodness or God's goodness, a Fruit of the Spirit,[147] is a direct correlation to "a positive quality characterized by an interest in the welfare of others and frequent generosity."[148] Goodness in its most generic form is acting on the behalf and welfare of others, without concern or regard for oneself. Several servant leadership characteristics align with leader goodness: (a) healing—helping others achieve a sense of being or recovering from a crisis event, (b) growth of people—purposeful and intentionally helping others to grow and succeed, (c) stewardship—putting others first, (d) ethical behavior—demonstrating authentic behavior characteristics.[149] As discussed earlier, trust is foundational to the leader and organizational success. When trust is evident in a relationship, goodness begins to emerge in leaders and followers, resulting in character development and growth. Leaders who live a life of character will seek the best for their followers, even at personal sacrifice or cost. Seeking the good in others will ultimately result in performance growth and organizational outcomes success. A person of character "is one who remains steadfast in their moral convictions, creeds, and codes, even if being steadfast to those convictions can lead to detrimental personal outcomes."[150]

While a leader can employ and practice the virtues and characteristics of contemporary theories such as transformational and servant leadership, character is often developed through arduous and long-term challenges or difficulties. However, even during hardship, a leader of character will persist in doing good and striving for success in the face of significant odds not in their favor. Academic research and author Angela Duckworth calls this "true grit."[151] In her research and work experience as a teacher in public schools, she found that

---

[147] Gal. 5:22–23 (NIV).
[148] Borcarnea, Henson, Huizing, Mahan, and Winston, 84.
[149] Joseph and Winston, 1.
[150] Wright and Emich, 1.
[151] (Duckworth 2013).

her highest performing students did not have the highest IQ or were considered the smartest. She found that the students who had the least, meaning those least privileged financially or educationally, and who worked the hardest in the most challenging circumstances, were likely to be the most successful over time. The predictor of success was not physical appearance, IQ, or privilege; it was grit.

In her terms, grit has the passion and persistence to achieve long-term goals. These innate behaviors to accomplish a challenging goal or objective is formed over time, with both frequent successes and setbacks, molding and creating a solid and resilient character of the leader and follower. Grits means staying focused on the future outcome of success. The most successful people are the ones who have the least and build character through grit. To build grit, a "growth mindset" is an approach that helps people adopt a position accepting failure when it occurs, learning from it, but then rising above, and continuing to pursue the goal or mission.

The last character trait a leader must have clarity is what do they want to be known for? Meaning, are they authentic, do they evaluate and examine circumstances and situations before taking action, and finally, do they clarify their code of ethics and live by them daily? For example, during World War II, the United States Military would capture enemy combatants and secure them in prisoner of war (POW) camps. Those combatants who were injured were treated in American hospitals by American doctors while a POW. This act of human compassion demonstrated the American value of human life. Even though war was fully underway with thousands of casualties across both sides, those countries who disagreed with the United States' position during the war still decided to align with the US because we held close values to human life. This behavior spoke to the testament and character of the United States government and military leadership, even during a global war.

As stated prior, a leader must purposefully decide they want to grow and develop positive characteristics through changing behaviors, attitudes, and approaches with those they lead. Character development begins with a transformation of the leader's heart and sacrificing for those they lead. To change, a leader must examine themself and call out precisely what they or others feel needs to be changed for their good and those they lead. The actual test of one's character is not only doing the right thing in front of others to see or hear from a leader but displaying the right behaviors and actions when no one is looking or observing. Today's organizations and society, in general, are expecting and demanding greater integrity and character of leaders across political, economic, and social arenas. While the journey begins with change, it requires continuous improvement and refining over time. It is not enough for leaders to just achieve character; it takes just as much effort to maintain consistency throughout their leadership journey, especially during tumultuous times.

Examples of Leaders of High Character

This section will highlight examples of leaders known as leaders of high character in political office and the airline's industry.

Theodore Roosevelt (twenty-sixth president of the United States)

"For the nation and the individual, the one indispensable requisite is character—There is no more important component of character than steadfast resolution. A man must do good. He must be brave and energetic; he must be resolute and persevering" (https://blog. traillifeusa.com/character-and-success).

Theodore Roosevelt, the twenty-sixth president of the United States, was born on October 27, 1858, and died January 6, 1919. He was an "American original," a man of high character to the American people and foreign allies.[152] His character and leadership approach embodied confidence, trust, compassion, empathy, honesty, and duty to the Nation. His resolve was to always make the right decisions for the right reasons and seldom was in error. In his lifetime, he achieved many goals such as mastering six foreign languages, writing and publishing over forty books, learned to fly a plane and lead-

---

[152] Lodice, 8

ing the Panama canal's construction. The list of accomplishments he achieved in his lifetime could continue. However, what shaped his character to make him the man and reviled leader he became? What servant leadership characteristics did he exemplify? These questions will be addressed below.

President Roosevelt's life journey was not without struggle and setbacks. He was born into sickness with asthma and other illnesses preventing him from public school and requiring home school instruction. In his youth, he developed a great appreciation for nature and animals. Later in his teens, he developed his physical abilities as a star athlete, pushing himself to excel and improve from the previous day consistently. Roosevelt attributes much of his upbringing to his father, as he said, "My father, Theodore Roosevelt, was the best man I ever knew. He combined strength and courage with gentleness, tenderness, and great unselfishness. He would not tolerate in us children selfishness or cruelty, idleness, cowardice, or untruthfulness."[153] These characteristics embedded into Roosevelt would later manifest in his leadership capabilities, which align with servant leadership virtues of altruism, empathy, trust, and love of people. Roosevelt believed in the equality of all people. For example, early on in his presidency, he was the first president to invite Booker T. Washington, an African-American, to dine with him in the White House. This was unheard of, yet it displayed his compassion and desire to show love and acknowledge other American's who were not of the same ethnicity. While he received much protest and resistance from those who did not agree with this approach, he persevered and knew this was the right step to help unify the American people.

Later on, he would continue in college at Harvard University, graduating magna cum laude and then choosing to enter politics fighting against social injustice and political corruption. While he rose in office in New York City politics, he was known as fierce and honest in his leadership while in office, further strengthening his character as a bold and committed leader of excellence. During this

---

[153] (Carleton 1958).

time, tragedy would strike him again with the death of his wife while delivering their second child. Despite this unfortunate life event, he chose to persevere in his political leadership as NYC Police commissioner and, later, other higher-ranking national political offices such as the assistant secretary of the Navy.

In April 1898, the United States found itself at war with Spain. Roosevelt resigned from his high political position, which he did not have to leave, and began a volunteer Calvary Regiment called the Rough Riders to fight in the war effort. Because of his prior experience in the NY National Guard, he was able to teach and train the young men the necessary skills to fight with dignity and honor. Here again, Roosevelt's character came forth in his leadership as a commander and his service to his men who were from all walks of life (college graduates, cowboys, hunters, prior service members, Native Americans, etc.) under him. Through his leadership, he demonstrated many servant leadership virtues of love of all people and service to those in his command. After the war, he again continued his political career as governor of New York, vice president, and eventually, president of the United States(Lodice 2017)(Lodice 2017). Roosevelt was the first American president to achieve the highest political office at forty-two and ten months. His idealized influence and inspirational motivation as a transformation leader and servant leader characteristics gained him notoriety and respect as a man of high caliber and character. Roosevelt was consistent in his actions and behaviors, dedicated to hard work, and a continual desire to help people.

Chelsy Sullenburger, speaker, safety advocate,
retired military and US Airways pilot

"A consummate leader who takes pride in living a life of integrity in both personal and business endeavors" (http://www.sullysullenberger.com/).

US Airways Captain Chelsy Sullenberger, is famously known for landing flight 1549 or "Miracle on the Hudson" on the Hudson River on a cold Wintery day in New York on January 15, 2009. Sullenberger is a thirty-year veteran pilot, retired Air Force pilot, safety instructor, and advocate for aviation safety (Captain Chesley "Sully" Sullenberger retires from US airways. 2010)(Captain Chesley "Sully" Sullenberger retires from US airways. 2010). His actions and behaviors and the entire flight crew saved the lives of over two hundred people on the plane bound for Charlotte, North Carolina. Captain Sullenberger is a servant leader because of his unwavering commitment to excellence in his work and his passion for serving and ensuring airline safety for others to learn and benefit. What made him perform flawlessly? How can others learn and employ his approach to servant leadership, service to others, especially during a climatic event?

Captain Sullenberger began his career as an aviator during his formative years growing up flying small planes. He also attended the Air Force Academy and flew fighter jets with a commitment to excellence, always preparing and practicing for the future. He served his country with honor and respect. After retiring, he then began a civilian pilot career with US Airways, which is now American Airlines. Again, he focused on always preparing and planning for future scenarios, developing and refining his behavior characteristics. Captain Sullenberger did not expect to land a plan on the Hudson River. Still, because of his years of continual practice and desire to always display the right behaviors and actions, no fatalities occurred.

Sullenberger demonstrated servant leadership during this entire event. For example, he was the last person to get off the plane, ensuring the safety of everyone. Then after ensuring everyone was off, he aided a passenger by giving his coat to them who were freezing and going into shock while waiting for emergency response service to arrive. For any profession, skills predict behavior for a known situation. However, neither the captain nor the plane was equipped to land on water. Yet his character traits of excellence and focus became the central theme of his success. Sullenberger knew the virtues of flying a plane while embodying "more general virtues of courage, restraint, cool judgment, and determination to do the right thing for others."[154] Imagine if the pilot was a newly graduated aviator who did not have the years of experience or knowledge the captain possessed? Or suppose it was a veteran pilot of ten years but did not practice scenarios over and over before this flight? Very likely, this would have been a disastrous situation with untold casualties. What Sullenburger invoked during this emergency landing was second nature behavior characteristics. First nature is stopping and asking, what is the right following step action or task? During the flight of 1949, Sullenberger did not have the luxury to ask what is the right thing to do. He made decisions automatically in split seconds when the jet's motors failed from Canadian geese entering the engines until the final landing. This is the challenge, how to help others achieve second nature behavior characteristics over time, so their behaviors and actions are flawless. How is second nature behavior achieved? Through commitment of practicing, over and over, small and incremental tasks with excellence and purpose to improve from the previous day.

Captain Sullenberger, now retired, also espoused servant leadership characteristics of the growth of others for their good and benefit. Besides his heroic landing, he has been dedicated to the pursuit of safety his entire adult life, promoting aviation safety in the industry and abroad. His instant success and notoriety did not come with its challenges and personal sacrifice. For example, "In the month's aft er Sullenberger brought the crippled jetliner and its 155 passengers to a safe landing on the Hudson, he suffered from nightmares, insomnia, and post-traumatic stress symptoms.[155] Sullenberger always put safety first of his passengers and then looked to the bigger picture of security for all people, an exemplary leader with stellar character for others to learn and emulate.

---

[154] Wright, 21.
[155] Rainey, 16.

Insights on Examples

Roosevelt lived a life of service to the American people and those who reported and followed him. What made Roosevelt great was not his political or social achievements but his focus on always competing with himself, making himself better the next day, growing his leadership traits and skills. His resolve of excellence and passion for honesty, trust, and truthfulness in all his interactions is what made him a great servant leader. Similarly, Chelsy Sullenberger also lived a life of service from an early age through his retirement. Both of these men did not seek notoriety; however, they did seek moral and ethical treatment of all people. They also saught excellence in their lives pursuits no matter the task or challenge. Despite setbacks, they always dared to face another day and advocate for others well being and goodness, traits of servant leaders.

An interview with Dr. Barry Doublestein, college professor, author, nonprofit board member

Dr. Barry A. Doublestein received his bachelor of arts (BA) from Albion College, a master of arts in educational administration from Truman State University, and a doctorate of strategic leadership (DSL) from the School of Business and Leadership at Regent University. He is an adjunct professor of Leadership in the School of Business and Leadership at Regent University where he teaches strategy development in the masters of organizational leadership program, leadership theory and communication, and healthcare leadership in the doctor of strategic leadership program. He has been president and chief operating officer of the Osteopathic Institute of the South in Grayson, Georgia, since 1989. He is president of Leadership Solutions (a medical education and leadership consulting firm). He is chairman of the board for the Georgia-based not-for-profit Peace Mountain Enterprises. He served as chief of Governmental Relations for the Georgia Osteopathic Medical Association for over ten years, and he is a former clinical associate professor in the Department of Family Medicine at Kiram Patel College of Osteopathic Medicine and clinical assistant dean for clinical education for the Georgia Track. Additionally, he taught healthcare administration at Belhaven University, Atlanta/Chattanooga.

Dr. Doublestein is passionate about physician-professionalism development programs and is a long-term consultant with the Duke University Medical School Department of Head and Neck Surgery and Communication Sciences on training residents and healthcare team members in the necessary skills to attain the highest level of professionalism possible. He has published numerous articles and book chapters and spoken internationally on the issue of self-leadership and the role it plays in professionalism development.

In his private time, Dr. Doublestein loves to discover more about his family ancestry, restore cars and boats, and is building a kit airplane in his shop. His greatest joy is spending time with his wife, children, and eleven grandchildren.

When you hear the word character, what comes to mind? How would someone describe your character, and why? I agree with Oz Guinness's position on character to which he speaks in his book: *When No One Sees: The Importance of Character in an Age of Image.* He describes character as the "inner form that makes anyone or anything what it is—whether a person, a wine, or a historical period." He states that it is "distinct from such concepts as personality, image, reputation, or celebrity…it is the essential 'stuff' from which one is made…their inner reality in which thoughts, speech, decisions, behavior, and relations are rooted (p. 16)." Character is deeper than prevailing philosophies, cultural mores, traditions, political movements.

One's worldview (how they make sense of their experience, in essence it is an accounting…an audit that brings balance to the equation…what goes in goes out) emanates from their character. Today, the world is okay with the philosophy of dualism in which there is a separation between what one is in public compared to their private behaviors. To the student of character, this is abhorrent for it is no different than how much of the World views Christians…merely hypocrites…saying one thing and doing another. This is a problem for the leader, for study after study finds that the most admirable leaders are those who live their character…they are the same inside and out…and can be counted upon regardless.

In my estimation, this is the single most important characteristic of great leaders…they are people of character…consistent, committed to death, and uncompromising. In fact, Robert Quinn defines leadership as not being about outcomes or results, rather it is about commitment…as he says: *it means to go forth to die.* I like this concept that leading others is not about what one might attain from the power differential of leader…follower, rather it is about the leader being of such character that all that matters is elevating others around them to be the best they could ever be…by taking them to a place they would never go on their own…that is leadership. Kouzes and Posner suggest that leadership is about credibility…that simply does not happen unless the leader is of virtuous character…always… never wavering.

So the important question to ask is…as long as a person is of consistent character is that all that matters? No, in fact, the quality of a person's character is what matters. For example, a winemaker might make a wine of consistent character…but if that character is the taste of rotten fruit…it is useless. So every character must be based upon its foundation. Here is the problem for today's leaders…holding to a set of standards in today's post-modern, relativistic society is WRONG because it is seen as judgmental if someone doesn't agree with those standards. 'Who are you to judge another…after all, we are not supposed to judge people… Jesus said it himself.' This view is a perversion of Jesus' intent…he was speaking clearly about calling others out for something they are doing willfully…being hypocrites. Every day…each and every one of us judges…it is called discriminating between options…for example, I judge whether I should wear formal clothing or jeans to a dinner party. On the basis of certain evidence, I make a decision. The evidence from which I make the clothing decision depends on the expectations of the host of the dinner. If their expectation was formal attire and I chose to wear jeans, I disrespect the host and the others attending the party who chose formal wear. Even though I have the 'right' to wear jeans, I do not because of its impact upon others. What if I don't like formal wear?

The only choice of the person of virtuous character is to wear it or not attend.

When we speak of virtuous character, to what are we specifically referring? There is a certain set of basic qualities of well-being that have been universally accepted across all cultures, people groups, nations, tongues, and tribes for thousands of years. These qualities, when lived consistently, regardless of circumstances or potential outcomes, result in good. Virtuously good character, when practiced, instills trust and credibility and attracts followers. So how does this relate to leading any organization (secular or sacred)? For an organization to operate in a unified and congruent manner, it must hold to a certain set of virtues that is accepted by *everyone* within the organization. This is important for in order to operate effectively, there must be a certain set of 'agreed-upon qualities' through which everything is filtered. Many people throw around the integrity word. Being a person of integrity can be defined differently by various groups, so, how can that virtue be used to form the 'virtuous character' of that organization? This is where the leader is responsible to specifically define the term in light of the organization. In healthcare, integrity means doing what one says they will do. The excellent virtuous leader of character will hold everyone within the organization to the standard of doing what they promise…never wavering…even when it might hurt or cost money. It boils down to consistency…in thought and action…*every time, everywhere.*

How do you keep your character in check, and how are you continuing to grow your character? If I were a narcissist, it would be nearly impossible to keep my character in check. It is about recognizing and ordering my life around the concept that the World does not operate as I will it to be. It is about willfully placing limits upon my actions… being conscious that my behavior always results in consequences for those around me. Those consequences can be good or bad. I live by a certain set of "no-goes," things that I have determined from years of engaging with others that I would *never* do…regardless of who is watching. These are my first-principles…long-beforehand determined.

I have learned that violation of these first principles will bring disgrace or harm to those directly impacted by my choice, and maybe even people I have never met. I have determined that living consistently brings peace, trust, and joy to those around me. I consider my audience (those watching me) and how they might be strengthened or weakened as a direct result of my behavior or actions. For example, I know that I am a servant of the Lord Jesus Christ, and when I live as I may want…it will diminish him in the eyes of others. My goal in life is to stand before him some day just to hear six simple words: 'Well done good and faithful servant.' I am also a husband to Vivian. I want to make her better and I cannot do that if I am living an immoral life seeking my own pleasures. I am a father to three married children with spouses who desire that I live a consistent life of good virtue. I also am a grandfather to eleven grandchildren that need to see a model of someone who chooses to live virtuously. I am also a professor who must live what I teach…so that my students can see theory in action. I am a friend to many and they need to see me live consistently.

The worse thing that could result from my behavior is to violate my first principles…that alone keeps my character in check. So every day, every moment of my life, I filter all of my response actions through this virtuous character filter. Do I make mistakes from time to time? Yes, but I learn from those mistakes…making a decision to not error in the same manner again when placed in the same situation.

What areas do you see today's organization needing in terms of character development and sustainability? An organization without a clear sense of their virtues will fail. Nothing is more important for a leader than to clearly develop and articulate virtuous character. If the leader is not of good virtuous behavior or is ignorant of its importance or existence, the entire organization suffers in purpose and action. A nonvirtuous leader will produce a nonvirtuous culture. I once worked in the marketing division for an organization whose chairman was having an affair with a vice president while both were married. While I was meeting with potential clients, many asked if the leader was still sleeping with the vice president. To the potential client, the character (or lack thereof) mattered.

It has been said that what parents accept of their children in moderation will lead to them practicing excess. If a leader exhibits (accepts) nonvirtuous behavior (even in their own life), others throughout the organization will find other ways to excessively live nonvirtuously. How the leader lives provides permission for equal or worse behavior across the board.

What are our recommendations for leaders to build and grow their character? How would this also apply to the organization they lead and serve? A virtuous leader *must* make it very clear to *everyone* in the organization what will be the first-principles upon which everything will be tested or evaluated. This must be *continuous* and must be transparent to *everyone* both within and without the organization.

Practical Application

As highlighted in this chapter through both definitions and several examples, character is often formed through hardships, setbacks, and how a leader or follower approaches a circumstance or issue. Developing and nurturing sound character traits requires time, life experiences, and a willingness to learn, especially from frequent failure. The character of a person, no matter role or responsibility, is tied directly to how they think, which manifests itself into behaviors and actions. However, how can today's modern leader, especially servant leader, grows and develops character in their workplace? Today's global arena requires courageous and dynamic leadership. The following recommendations below, while not exclusive or in any specific order, will help both current and new leaders strengthen and affirm their character attributes. Character is developed over time, with willful and purposeful intentions to change for the leader's good and those they routinely interact with.

Develop inner iron (resilience)

Most character development occurs over many years of interactions where leaders face insurmountable odds or challenges that push them to abandon their cause or purpose. However, when a leader or follower embraces difficulty and acknowledges the challenge, they have begun to turn the tide of their situation and see what can be done to grow and develop their character. Theodore Roosevelt could have chosen not to continue in his political career. Still, his deep desire to do more extraordinary things as a leader who believed in excellence and overcoming a challenge developed his true grit. Second, a leader should examine their motives for the cause they are advocating or defending. In other words, what benefits will come forth as a result of a leader's willingness to expound energy and make personal sacrifices? Third, remaining calm and patient amid conflict and crisis will help a leader with clarity of thought and make the right decisions based on the current circumstances. Fourth, a leader should keep the goal of what they are trying to achieve consistently front and center, especially if many others align with similar purpose and intent. Always cast a vision of the future for everyone else to see and join in.

Remain humble and true to purpose (staying grounded)

Humbleness, is keeping one's ambitions and self-glorification in check, meaning putting others first above personal gain and achievement. Leaders must look beyond their personal advance and put those they lead ahead of themselves for their good and benefit. How is humility developed and practiced? First, build a culture of inclusion where continually stating "we" instead of "I." A leader should take the focus off of themself and build others up in word and action. Second, a leader should remain remain connected to those they interact with on a daily basis. Being present and attentive in conversations will build trust and confidence, especially with those who are going through difficult situations. Staying grounded is living out the virtues of servant leadership discussed earlier.[156]

---

[156] (Barton 2019).

Staying true to your convictions (courage)

During times of difficulty, a leader's true character and leadership ability are often exposed and experienced by those they lead. To develop courage, a leader must remain true to their decisions and actions. Being decisive and acting, even if resulting in negative consequences, develops confidence and courage over time. While the author of this manuscript is not encouraging action for the sake of action, however learning from failures, and returning to the arena of the circumstance, builds courage. Also, remain vulnerable in your thoughts and actions. In other words, ask for help or input in times of uncertainty, yet remain confident in a final decision, especially if others will be impacted. Second, make decisions that are the right ones for those you serve, even if it is not a popular choice or considered a quick solution to an issue. A leader will always be judged by their inner convictions. Those organizations that empower their leaders to think, take risks, and make decisions are generally "higher-performing organizations."[157]

Living out your principles

A leader must be intentional in their word and actions. Like courage, they must control their thoughts and actions by inhibiting the right behaviors and exposure to similar leaders you aspire and admire. What a leader thinks, manifests itself in personality and character. For example, develop friendships and mentor relationships with those who portray and live out similar core values and principles. Develop a network or inner circle of friends who will hold you accountable to your core values. Encourage others to hold you responsible. Engage in learning environments such as college courses, webinars, and publications that further develop and strengthen your core values. Develop and self-discipline your mind to remain focused on your principles, especially during distractions or crisis events.

---

[157] Barton, 5.

Assume responsibility and ownership

A leader must be accountable and responsible for their word and actions. They must make clear thier intentions so that you are held accountable and responsible to those you interact with. Set specific guidelines as to what you feel is a character trait that is important for you. In other words, accept your shortcomings and be open and honest to change. When a goal or project is not completed to satisfaction, acknowledge where this could have done better and seek to improve this over time. A leader should encourage others to push and motivate them to continually improve performance and their character.

Willingness to sacrifice

A key characteristic of a servant leader is self-sacrifice for the betterment of others. A leader builds integrity with those they lead out of their self-sacrifice. An example would be a manager giving up their bonus or promotion so their followers will receive their yearly performance compensation and also receive promotion. A second example is a leader who gives up their training budget to continue in their education and growth. A third is a leader who disregards their contributions to a successful project or goal and purposefully promoting others who were involved in receiving full acknowledgment above themself. All of these actions can manifest themselves in their unique way within the workplace.

Develop spiritual connectivity

Having a spiritual connection is just as vital as living out the characteristics of servant leadership. A leader should put in place a time for daily reflection and inner solace to connect with God. Purposefully set a time of day for a specific duration, typically in the morning, to reflect on the goodness and blessings of God and seek with anticipation what he will do in the future. Spiritual awareness develops a mindset of making wise decisions that will benefit a leader and those they love around them.

Respect and honor others

Love, or *Agapeo Love*, according to Winston (2002) "is the Greek term for moral love, meaning doing the right thing at the right time and for the right reasons."[158] Respecting and honoring others is a form of love. When a leader or follower acknowledges someone else in a moral and respectful way, they show love and do the right thing. In this manner, relationships begin to grow, and in tandem, a leader's character develops. For example, when meeting someone for the first time or in a meeting, give the other person opportunity to complete their thoughts and then respectfully ask to respond accordingly, especially if a topic or concept is being debated. The first few minutes of meeting a new person you may have never engaged with before will set the expectations and thoughts of your character in their minds. Those initial meetings of showing respect and honor to others will set the course for future interactions that will lead to either successes or failures.

---

[158] Patterson, 3.

CHAPTER 8

Love: The Primary Ingredient
of Servant Leadership

Today's modern leaders, especially servant leaders, are always seeking new and innovative ways to motivate and inspire the people to perform their best all times. Love, often thought of as an emotion or passion outside of the workplace, plays a vital role in motivating and developing leaders and followers to achieve excellence in their work and transcends to a changed life-impacting all those they interact with. "Loving leadership is fruitful leadership."[159] How does love immerge and manifest itself in organizations? Why is love a vital cornerstone of all leaders who seek success for themselves and their followers? This section will cover the definition of love for leaders and their followers, what it means to show love at work, examples of modern-day leaders who demonstrate love at work, an interview with a leader on their views of love at work, and finally, practical application examples.

The word and concept of love is the most discussed topic more than any other since the origins of time. Out of love, God created Eve as a helper to Adam, companionship, and pro-create and filling the world with people (Gen. 2:18). Out of love, people form bonds and

---

[159] Borcarnea, Henson, Huizing, Mahan, and Winston, 7.

everlasting relationships. Spears states, "Love is a powerful, healing, renewing, and fulfilling emotion."[160] Love brings forth goodness in people never displayed or experienced before. Love changes people's emotions, attitudes, and behavior to seek goodness—God's goodness—in others, despite how someone is treated. Love is on display when a leader or follower purposely goes out of there way, especially in sacrifice of oneself for the betterment of another. While Patterson (2003) brings forth the seven virtuous constructs of servant leadership: (1) love, (2) humility, (3) altruism, (4) vision, (5) trust, (6) empowerment, and (7) service, love is the overarching virtue a leader must live out with all they engage with for effectiveness. This type of love is a selfless giving of oneself for the success and development of others along life's journey. Loving servant leadership is not just a model or approach; it is a way of life lived out in every daily encounter with other human beings, no matter location or region.

Leaders must live by example, setting the vision, modeling the way, and setting expectations in their pursuit of success for their followers while in tandem keeping a line of sight with organizational objectives. However, if a leader spends the time investing in their followers to help them achieve what Greenleaf calls a state of being or self-actualization, organizational goals and objectives are often achieved. For example, if a leader displays and lives out their expectations of service excellence, their authentic behavior and actions will motivate followers to take on similar behaviors and actions. Leadership by example is decisive, it can either transcend followers to achieve success or cause failure if not appropriately demonstrated and modeled. A servant leader must display unconditional love to all people, regardless of their "inadequacies, disfigurements, racial and ethical differences."[161]

Most people, no matter their race or origin, have love within their inner being. Spears states, "Love is the healing, unifying, integrating, stimulating, renewing, reassuring, and constructive life force

---

[160] Spears, 50.
[161] Greenleaf, 50.

at the core of all good things. Without it, we have violence, destruction, confusion, and more."[162] Today's workplace needs a continual introduction and strengthening of love to help all people achieve fulfillment in their work and personal lives. How does a leader introduce love and keep it alive and vibrant? The leader must take the time to understand each employee's needs, wants, and desires. While this is no easy task and often takes months if not years to invest, the dividends of a changed life for the follower's good, are worth the time and self-sacrifice. The leader first focuses on the needs of the follower, then discovering their unique gifts and talents, and then determines how this can be intertwined into achieving organizational objectives. To attain a loving and fruitful relationship, the leader must be present and engage with their followers, showing care, compassion, and support. The leader must be "emotionally, physically, and spiritually present for the follower."[163]

Through unconditional love of people, a leader will have faith and hope in their followers to perform their best. When they display less than satisfactory results, they extend grace for another chance to recover and learn from prior experiences. A leader will make space for healing and growth, seeking the good in their followers. Gratitude must always be at the core of every leader; it binds faith, hope, and love, the love of all people together. Given today's organizational climate of tensions and conflicts, coupled with current social, economic, and political upheaval that seems to increase as time progresses, there has never been a greater need for leaders to epitomize love, both in the workplace and the communities where they reside.

Conflict in society, has existed since Adam and Eve ate the forbidden fruit in the Garden of Eden.[164] Today, conflict is ever-present in almost every form of communication that leaders and followers employ. The question of conflict between individuals or groups of people is not if conflict will occur, but more so when it will happen. Conflict, primarily between two individuals, arises from dif-

---

[162] Spears, 51.
[163] Patterson, 3.
[164] Gen. 3:6 (NIV).

ferent expectations, perceptions, or beliefs about what is morally or ethically right. While conflict leads to questioning and evaluating other's viewpoints, it can strengthen and develop servant leadership behaviors of love through respect for another's position, showing care, demonstrating compassion, listening, and empathy. While conflict is unavoidable, one approach leaders can employ is "functional conflict."[165] as means to resolving issues or dilemmas with diverse and disparate groups as opposed to dysfunctional conflict. In this manner, "Functional conflict leads an organization to challenge assumptions, innovate, and think creatively while dysfunctional conflict can be costly and destructive."[166] Functional conflict requires an investment of a leader into their followers "for good intrapersonal and interpersonal relations in organizations."[167] This provides a balance between follower needs, desires, and wants while still achieving positive organizational outcomes. Effective leaders will find equilibrium between the needs of their team and the expected goals and priorities of the organization.

All people have an innate desire and need to be loved. This desire includes what Patterson calls a moral and respective love of people, acknowledging each other as a human being first, above all else in common or not in common. "Love is the source from which virtuous leadership comes."[168] A leader's love of people motivates followers to align with the leader's vision, transcending above any personal agendas, differences, or opposition for the good of the organization and its mission. Love can establish and build relationships beyond the transactional engagements of followers being financially rewarded for their efforts to where the follower excels in performance for the leader's good and the organization they serve. *Agape* love is a continual giving love that seeks no form or reciprication from another other than to replicate that same love to others. Hoehner states, agape love "It is not a love of the worthy, and it is not a love that desires to pos-

---

[165] Borcarnea, Henson, Huizing, Mahan, and Winston, 8.

[166] Borcarnea, Henson, Huizing, Mahan, and Winston, 8–9.

[167] Kudonoo, Schroeder, and Boysen–Rotelli, 52.

[168] Borcarnea, Henson, Huizing, Mahan, and Winston, 9.

sess. On the contrary, it is a love given quite irrespective of merit, and it is a love that seems to give."[169] To love someone is to place oneself in service to others and mutually serve each other in group settings.

To show and purposely behave lovingly to others at all times is a choice, especially when it requires doing the right act or seeking what is best for others' good or benefit. This approach "involves continually making choices for the highest benefit of others… This is an integrated approach of love toward others because it involves continuity and learning."[170] However, fear, not love, leads to accelerated conflict, anxiety, confusion, frustration, and dysfunctional behaviors. A leader's love of followers inspires hope, confidence, and a deep and strong connection that will withstand sudden changes or unexpected crisis events in the workplace, such as the recent COVID-19 global pandemic.

A leader's love, especially a servant leader's love of their followers, is so strong in force and impact that it changes and transforms the hearts and character of their followers. "The force of love is so great that it can cause leaders to lead with understanding, gratitude, kindness, forgiveness and compassion."[171] When a leader invests in the follower to understand their passions and desires, there begins a beautiful relationship that naturally motivates the follower to engage with increased vigor and a love of their work. While fear and coercion of a leader will produce short-term results, love is more effective and achieves both short and long-term objectives. Effective leadership will only emerge when the leader gives selflessly to all those they interact with, ensuring they meet the needs and desires of their followers.[172]

Loving leadership creates a culture of unity and oneness amongst all people, despite differences and viewpoints. Developing a culture of love requires creating an environment where the very nature and act of love are continually on display for all to see and experience, cre-

---

[169] Hoehner, 709.
[170] Miller, 96.
[171] Dierendonck and Patterson, 72.
[172] (Engstrom 1976).

ating a loving atmosphere at all times. A loving leadership approach to organizational design and strategy will create a culture of long-lasting and sustained relationships. "A culture of love is best understood as mutual care and consideration between leaders and followers whereby individual perspectives and contributions are appreciated, and members have a sense of collective commitment to the organization and each other."[173] When this culture begins to form, it opens new synergies, innovations, and thought processes never experienced before, creating a spirit of achieving the impossible.

Examples of Leaders Who Exemplified Love in Leadership

This section will highlight examples of leaders who have demonstrated and practiced love as a primary leadership principle.

Ross Perot (American business magnate, billionaire, presidential candidate, former naval officer, and philanthropist)

"Lead and inspire people. Don't try to manage and manipulate people. Inventories can be managed, but people must be led" (https://www.rossperot.com/quotes-and-books).

Henry Ross Perot was born June 27, 1930, in Texarkana, Texas, and died July 9, 2019. Perot was known for his deep care and loyalty to his employees at Electronic Data Systems (EDS), a company he founded.[174] His life spanned many years in leadership. First, beginning as a graduate of the United States Naval Academy and serving as a naval officer, then through several other global organizations such as International Business Machines (IBM) in sales leadershp roles, starting Electronic Data Systems (EDS), serving as founder and chief executive officer, and later on, becoming a philanthropist.[175]

Perot believed in persistence and the value of character. He served eight years in the Navy who espoused a solid and committed

---

[173] Borcarnea, Henson, Huizing, Mahan, and Winston, 14.
[174] (Koulopoulos 2019).
[175] (Stone 2019).

work ethic that helped him achieve succes and his desire to help others achieve their potential. After serving the nation, he demonstrated his deep love for the United States and all those served by remembering prisoner of wars (POWs) who sacrificially gave their lives in service. He always took care of and acknowledged American troops for their service and his employees in all of his organizations.[176] Perot took the time to invest in his people and cared deeply for them. For example, in 1979, two of his employees were taken hostage by the Iranians. He financially funded and organized a rescue operation, freeing these two Americans.

He was known for his positive attitude and charisma, always focused on doing the right thing for the customer and his employees, a man of authenticity. For example, during most weekends, his organization would conduct exercises with his leadership to verify the whereabouts of all his employees across the globe, ensuring their safety and well-being, making sure they felt safe and loved. This demonstrated his love throughout the organization as he knew his employees might be in harm's way at times, but wanted to let them know he cared for them at all times.

Perot was also known for always espousing equality for all his employees. "Perot himself was fond of reminding people that if an associate's child needed medical attention at 2:00 a.m., they should be treated just like he'd want his own child treated."[177] This leadership approach in the love of people created a reciprocal bond in what Koulopoulos called fierce loyalty. During their executive meetings for his son Ross Jr. (CEO), it was prevalent to inquire about the health and well-being of his direct-report families. Perrot Sr. expected responses to validate just how well they were doing, validating his desire to show his care for them genuinely. This complete focus on people formed a culture of trust, deep loyalty, and agapeo love of self-sacrifice and giving in the organization.

---

[176] (Stilwell 2020).
[177] (Koulopoulos 2019).

His life mirrored that of a great humanitarian for others. As a young man, he learned from his mother to always help others, especially those less fortunate and under challenging circumstances. "You sit there in that little house in Texarkana and see your mother doing things like feeding the hungry when you're a child. That's the greatest lesson in the world" (https://www.rossperot.com/life-story/humanitarian). Later in his career, Perot began the Perot Foundation in 1969, focusing on many humanitarian and civic causes. His high energy spirit and deep desire to help others were evident through his foundation by giving several colleges for disease research, such as diabetes. He also personally acknowledged and celebrated two Nobel Prize winners in 1985 for their research in medicine by holding a ceremony honoring these two doctors for their efforts and success in medical research. In addition to many other financial gifts to medical research, he also focused on giving to the arts.

For example, he made donations to the Morton H. Meyerson Symphony Hall, the Dallas Museum of Art, the Dallas Arboretum, and began the Perot Museum of Nature and Science. Perot was also a significant supporter of the church his family workshiped in, the Highland Park Presbyterian Church, the North Texas Food Bank, the United Way, and many others.

He always believed in acknowledging all people. For example, as a senior leader in General Motors Company, he would follow around the factory managers and see if the line workers would look up at him and smile. When he found line workers ignoring or just nodding, he knew this was not a vibrant or happy culture where people wanted to work and spend their working days. However, when a factory worker would take the time to look up when he said, "Hey, Charlie, how are you?" that indicated a joyous spirit within the culture of the factory. This leadershp approach is what breeds commitment, loyalty, respect, and love that begins to develop between people, regardless of role or title.[178]

---

[178] (Perot 1996).

Perot truly understood that the workplace is where each member of the organization finds their purpose, meaning in life, identity within the organization, and how they would grow as human beings serving each other, not employees working just to collect a weekly paycheck. "It's a place that gives them the opportunity to be part of something much larger than themselves."[179] His love of those he led gave them something greater than themselves to participate in, seeking good in others and aspiring always to do better.

Jim Sinegal (American billionaire businessman, founder, and former CEO of Costco Wholesale Corporation)

"You destroy the initiative of the working people if they don't feel they have a fighting chance to be a part of the American Dream" (https://quotefancy.com/james-sinegal-quotes).

James D. Sinegal, born January 1, 1936, is a retired American billionaire businessman who co-founded Costco, a wholesale mega retail business based in Seattle, Washington, and led this organization as its chief executive officer (CEO) until retirement in 2012. During his reign as CEO, he, with his organization, was able to supersede competitor Sam's Club and BJ's Wholesale, becoming the most prominent wholesale operation in the United States, Harvard Business School. Senegal is noted as a leader in the retail industry through its progressive management practices, resulting in low employee turnover and high employee productivity. As CEO, he truly cared and loved his employees, putting them first in his leadership. He is known for his authentic leadership[180] approach to work, which will be discussed below.

Sinegal was raised in Pittsburgh, Pennsylvania, in a working-class family. In 1955, he began his work life as a grocery bagger for Fedmart grocery stores. His passion for the retail business grew and he moved up into various leadership roles, eventually becoming

---

[179] (Koulopoulos 2019).
[180] (Northouse 2013).

vice president of merchandising and operations. He worked as several other retail operations through the years and started Costo in 1983 with another retail executive, Jeff Brotman. Sinegal's leadership qualities and his love of people enabled his followers to accept his vision and path for the future.

Sinegal is known for: always focusing inward, valuing culture, leading from Costco store floors, listening to his employees, always remained available for them, practiced humility and humbleness, and sought to solve employee issues. While maintaining excellent customer service, he believed in a stable store environment for employees.[181] As CEO, he also believed culture was an essential element to success in the retail business. Culture defines what and who a leader and the organization they serve is, which develops integrity, honesty, passion, ownership amongst all in the organization. He felt that customers would gain trust in Costco when employees aligned with these values and become returning customers.

He also believed in frequent store visits across the country, making it a point to visit at least two hundred stores a year to understand his employees and ensure their needs were met. Sinegal always made himself available to his organization. For example, his main office was located right in the middle of a hallway with no door or glass to stop someone from entering in, removing obstacles for people to engage. He is a humble man with a common and down-to-earth approach to engaging with his organization. Even as CEO, he answered his own phone calls. Material wealth and assets were of no importance to him. Sinegal was known for being a great communicator, ensuring employees knew the plan of Costo and how this would impact them. During his time as CEO, he held in high regard a code of ethics and a simplistic approach to problems while valuing the opinions of both customers and employees.

Costco is a great place to work and is named one of the best organizations to work for in the United States. In 2017, Forbes named Costco America's Best Large Employer over Walmart and

---

[181] (Papia 2021).

Google. Much of this success is from Sinegal's leadership, ensuring employees are well taken care of with adequate compensation, generous benefits, and most of all, everyone is treated like family, an important quality of servant leadership.

As mentioned earlier, Jim Sinegal is considered an authentic leader is demonstrating his interpersonal qualities, connecting with his organization daily. For example, he felt he was equal to those who worked on the floor by wearing a name badge with only his first name "Jim" (www.sites.psu.edu). He understood his position and role in the organization to engage with his employees, not regarding himself as more significant than anyone else as a humble leader. "And when Sinegal walks into one of his stores, he's treated like a celebrity. His employees seem to like him genuinely. And the feeling's mutual. The employees know that I want to say hello to them because I like them."[182] This approach builds a strong culture of trust and love for each other. His early life experiences of retail work and his working-class upbringing and values were evident in the Costco culture.

His love for his followers became evident in their loyalty to him because he purposely paid higher wages and premium benefits than the competition in the retail industry. During the Great Recession of 2007, he deliberately made a commitment to his employees that no one would let go, and in fact, gave them a raise to help them during the financial crisis. This resulted in low employee turnover and a high rate of promotion from within. According to Sinegal, "There's a real business advantage to treating employees well, imagine that you have 120,000 loyal ambassadors out there who are constantly saying good things about Costco. It has to be a significant advantage for you," and "Wall Street is in the business of making money between now and next Tuesday," he said. "We're in the business of building an organization, an institution that we hope will be here 50 years from now. And paying good wages and keeping your people working with

---

[182] (Goldberg and Ritter 2006).

you is very good business."[183] This approach and philosophy made him a highly effective, respected, honored, and authentic leader.

Insights on Examples

Perot and Sinegal both deeply cared and loved their followers. While they both have a different approach and thought process to leadership with Perot leading EDS as a global technology company, and Sinegal leading Costco as a powerhouse mega retail store, they both always looked to the value of each individual in their respective organization. Their humble beginnings taught them giving and seeking the best in others was foundational for success. Their approaches completely align with the servant leadership virtues of love and service to all. They both believed in loyalty, trust, strong relationships, and family-oriented leadership styles, which embody servant leadership principles.

An Interview with Dr. Daniel Mundt, Minister,
National Coach, College President

Ministry leadership. Daniel Mundt serves as a National Coach for The Foursquare Church. Before accepting the role of a coach in 2021, Daniel served as the Heartland District supervisor. The Heartland District is made up of six Midwest states. Those states include Minnesota, Iowa, Wisconsin, Illinois, Michigan, and Indiana. Daniel's primary responsibilities in the Heartland District are to develop leaders and multiply and transform churches. Likewise, in December of 2019, Daniel accepted a role as acting college president of Life Pacific University in Christiansburg, Virginia. He served as acting president until March 2021. He has also served on boards and committees as a lead pastor, church planter, and support roles within the Foursquare Church.

---

[183] (Goldberg and Ritter 2006).

Education. Daniel graduated from Mt. Vernon Bible College (Ohio) in 1986 with a BA in theology and completed a master's degree in strategic leadership in 2015 (California). Daniel received a doctorate in strategic leadership (DSL) from Regent University (Virginia) in May 2020.

Family. Daniel and Cindy have been married for thirty-nine years and have been in Ministry Leadership together for thirty-two of those years. They are the proud parents of Joshua (twenty-nine) and Rebecca (twenty-six). In December 2020, their daughter and son-in-law Erick gave them their first grandchild—Indie June Recinos.

Why do you think love is a crucial virtue required of all leaders and followers? I believe that love is an *essential* virtue for effective leadership! Loving leadership is where people are more important than the task to be accomplished and achieving profit. People thrive in a context of love and acceptance. Without genuine care and empathy from the boss, the work becomes mundane and transactional. When the leader puts high value (love) on the follower (employer/employee), the follower is more motivated to help the leader accomplish the task and work hard for a more significant financial benefit for the organization.

Simply put, loved and valued people are more likely to treat people how they would be treated. Thus, the customer senses that they are valued and served with more outstanding excellence. Also, a leader/follower relationship is often hindered by the power distance between them. The follower can feel like their relationship is to accomplish the tasks or the job they are hired for. The leader can feel like they must use the power of their position to motivate the follower by criticism or lack of reward. Too often, we have witnessed when love is absent; the leader abuses the power they are entrusted with. However, when the leader is motivated by love for their followers, the power distance becomes more of a bridge than a barrier, a blessing than a curse. The follower senses this love and care and is freer to be authentic and bring their best self to the mission at hand.

Love and is a powerful word and takes on many forms in our relationships. Do you feel it is a requirement to love and serve those you lead? The word requirement is a difficult word to use when talking about love and a servant leader. I express this because the heart that loves the follower is born out of a sense of calling, is motivated intrinsically, and becomes a natural outflow of who the person is as a leader. This love grows as the leader becomes a servant over time. So I don't know if the servant leader would feel they are required to love the follower but instead, they chose to love as a way of leadership.

Can you clarify some of the specific qualities or character traits you admire and love about those you work with? The character traits and qualities I admire in those I work with are straightforward for me to name. I believe these qualities are longed for in organizations and leader-follower relationships today. These qualities and characteristics are the following:

- Humility: One who has a proper view of self
- Empathy: One who feels the pain of others and offers assistance
- Servant: One who puts followers first before the organization and their agenda
- Sponsor: One who sees the talent in others and uses their influence to advance them
- Collaborative: One who gets others involved in making decisions
- Listener: One who seeks feedback
- Foresight: Futuristic One who sees the big picture and has a long-term vision

How do you lead with love and service to others? What happens when the discussion involves corrective actions for a follower or is removed from their current role/responsibilities? What steps would you take? How do you show love and service, even in the most difficult circumstances and situations? I believe that love and service are vital traits for a leader when dealing with difficult people and having difficult confrontations. Much like the love and service of a father or mother when it comes time to discipline their child. Their discipline is motivated by love, and it puts the best interest of the person being disciplined about the convenience of not having a difficult conversation. Ultimately, love never fails in any situation. Even having to "let someone go" should be motivated by love and care for the person (s) involved.

Practical Application

Loving people is often one of the most challenging tasks a leader will encounter, especially during a difficult situation or when people are at odds with each other. Showing love to others may not be something a leader feels comfortable with or believes will undermine their authority or position as a stern and ever-demanding taskmaster. However, that mindset is the opposite of what the leader must do for a happy, vibrant, and highly productive workplace. Leading with love takes hard work, strategy, perseverance, and most of all, humility, putting others first above yourself. "Love in leadership has become an area of interest in many values-based leadership theories."[184] However, the application of love in the workplace can be daunting and challenging to achieve, especially in a short period. So where does a leader start? How do they begin to love all of their followers and all they engage with throughout their day? It all begins with a service mindset to others, no matter the task or expectation, helping them become better human beings for others to grow and develop. The following paragraphs will serve as a launching pad for leaders to open their hearts and souls to help their followers and themselves grow as influential and loving leaders.

Invest in the Lives of Your Followers

Take time to understand and learn about each of those with who you engage daily. This will require time and effort on the leader's part to personally commit to listening, caring, and understanding each follower's life story, including their desires and passions for the future. Wonderful and long-lasting relationships are often formed to serve both the leader and follower for future benefit. For example,

---

[184] Borcarnea, Henson, Huizing, Mahan, and Winston, 7.

purposely schedule a time during the week to have a conversation with each follower. Authenticity begins with the leader getting to know his followers personally and intimately through Agapeo Love. Work activities will likely come up; however, remain purposeful in your intention to build a relationship with your followers. There will be plenty of time always to discuss work. Take the time to learn about their spouses, children, and what stage of life they are in, and what they are looking forward to in the future. Think of each follower as a tree with many branches. It is unnecessary to understand every component but knowing a few of the main areas will yield much fruit for the relationship. As a leader, you learn their life stories, which most people are freely willing to share. They often desire a relationship with their leader to grow and achieve fulfillment in their work and life, what Greenleaf calls a "state of being."

Acknowledge their contributions to the organization

Followers want to be acknowledged in their work, even in the small things. Take time to notice what someone has done to help others or complete a task with excellence. Recognition contributes to a strong culture and builds a sense of oneness in the organization. It demonstrates a leader's attention to detail and builds camaraderie and team spirit. Kouzes and Posner posit two essential elements when acknowledging others: (1) expect the best and (2) personalize recognition.[185] How is this implemented? To expect the best, positively encourage others to achieve great things with excellence. Set the bar high in expectations, but ensure it is achievable within the time frame. Continually encourage people and help remove any roadblocks on the way to success. For example, when giving or assigning a project or task, ask yourself, as a leader, are the expectations realistic? Did I prepare them with the proper tools and equip them for success? Will this assignment challenge and stretch them to achieve greatness for themselves and all those around them? Second, personalizing rec-

---

[185] (Kouzes and Posner 2012).

ognition involves understanding what motivates each follower. This will likely require a significant amount of time for a leader to crack the coconut of the drivers that motivate each follower.

For example, when a follower comes up with a great idea, call this out in a weekly meeting verbally recognizing their efforts, then send an email to one of the senior leaders for acknowledgment with the follower copied highlighting their passion and innovation. Just don't send a thank-you email; make it personal, demonstrating understanding of the follower's idea. Praise is so essential for all to see and experience. Take time to celebrate work well done and milestone achievements. Purposely find a few highlights to call out to the team every week, being liberal in your praise of people. Always try to be creative and innovative in recognizing people. Indeed, this is no easy task; however, the fulfillment and joy a leader receives are worth the investment and sacrifice of their time and energy.

Purposefully verbalizing love

Strange and shocking as a leader may think, but verbalizing the words "I love you" to each follower will yield significant dividends that will continue to flow over the long-term. These words have a positive, creative, and almost magical effect on people. However, this approach should be kept in the proper context and clearly articulated so that all will understand the purpose and intent of Agapeo love. How does a leader demonstrate and apply to verbalize "I love you"? During team or organization meetings, verbally express love to everyone. Include this in Christmas cards, birthday wishes, and other celebratory times of the year. This does not need to be verbalized every day, but a routine and frequent reminder will suffice to build the loving and fruitful relationship needed to achieve success.

Leading in service

Leading in service is a complete focus on the follower for their success and growth as an individual. "Leaders model their service to others in their behavior, attitudes, and values."[186] How is this displayed in the workplace? Service is often seen through humility and altruism when the leader self-sacrifices their acknowledgment or financial gain for their followers. For example, a leader may decide to forfeit a raise or promotion for their follower to receive instead because they believed the follower deserved this acknowledgment. They may also give up coveted training they desired to take and allow the follower to participate and learn instead. Or they may pitch in and lead in a complex project or task that they did not have to engage in with the follower. They demonstrate courage and commitment to always remain available in time of need and show up focusing on the success of their followers, no matter the circumstance or the difficulty that lies ahead. This is the whole idea of self-giving sacrificial love, despite how a leader may feel or be treated by a follower.

Having fun and a joyous spirit

Loving leadership has one focus: to exalt and achieve fulfillment in the lives of the follower and the leader. This approach ignites creativity, motivates followers to do their best work, and allows followers to take risks without fear of repercussion or consequences. A leader must always foster fun in the workplace and have a joyous spirit for others to join in and share across the organization. For example, holding team meetings at a sports center such as Top Golf or sponsoring a Friday afternoon fun day for the team at an amusement park or cultural center will develop a spirit of fun. Doing something that is out of someone's normal behaviors or actions, to demonstrate their uniqueness that contributes to having fun, such as participating in a softball throw water dunking contest where people can take a chance to "dunk the boss." This will certainly generate passion and motivation to achieve the goal! They also engage in volunteering during work hours at local nonprofits serving the community, such as local schools, YMCAs, and Habitat For Humanity, to give back to the

---

[186] Dierendonck and Patterson, 172.

community and then acknowledging their challenging work by taking the team out to dinner to celebrate their accomplishments.

A joyous spirit must be evident in a leader's approach and style. While a leader faces difficulties and unexpected circumstances similar to followers, they must look beyond and always live a life of hope and improvement for a better tomorrow for themselves and their followers. "Loving leaders are joyful leaders."[187] When a leader shows up at work with a joyful spirit, followers will begin to align and display similar behaviors and attitudes. It is up the leader to set the tone and climate of the atmosphere for all to partake and join in. Joy shows up in many forms. An act or unexpected behavior can elicit joy. For example, when a leader brings in doughnuts for his team to enjoy or reward the team with dinner, including their spouses, creating a spirit of joy leads to fulfillment.

Being authentic

A leader must understand they are human, just like their followers. Humility, altruism, and compassion must be on display for others to see and experience. Authenticity requires a leader to remain highly ethical and known for living the right behaviors and positive leadership characteristics. While a clear and concise definition of authentic leadership is somewhat hard to encapsulate, leader authenticity is often seen and experienced through decisions and behavioral acts. Authentic leaders are not afriad to share they do not have all the answers and need the team's help to achieve its objectives Authenticity is also being genuine, honest, straightforward in communications, thinking through decisions before acting, and doing the right thing, despite the outcome. What are some examples that can be applied for authenticity? For example, asking for insights or feedback on a problem or issue from the team makes a leader more self-aware of their environment. Also, when delivering a difficult message such as layoffs or someone being terminated, communicate with genuine-

---

[187] Borcarnea, Henson, Huizing, Mahan, and Winston, 28.

ness and compassion, offering options as a next step. Seek the best or good in others, in all situations. Lead with the notion that it is good in everyone; it just requires discovery and the igniting of their goodness. Authenticity requires demonstrating a leader's human side, meaning poking fun at themselves and including humor in their behavior and attitude. Finally, authenticity requires humbleness and patience with their followers.

Patience is developed over several opportunities for the follower to recover from failure, learn from their experience, and build an authentic relationship with their leader. Finally, leaders should always look for opportunities to serve followers, such as identifying and meeting a personal need for the follower, finding career opportunities, and promotional opportunities to challenge further and advance themselves. Sometimes just a simple good morning or greeting is all that is required to demonstrate authenticity.

CHAPTER 9

360 Servant Leadership Assessment
for Leader Application

S ince the 1960s, servant leadership has become one of the most prolific and modern-day leadership approaches in academic writing and practice in organizations for improving organizational and individual performance. The following 360 servant leadership assessment will quickly help today's leader assess their leadership strengths and areas for improvement in their servant leadership approach. This will serve both a new leader and someone who has been in people manager roles for several years.

360 Degree Feedback Assessments have been used and implemented over the last twenty years to evaluate a leader or individual's strengths and areas for growth/improvement. "These employee assessments collect data from colleagues, subordinates, and clients—hence the name 360-degree appraisal—to help illuminate how well employees are performing and how individuals might need to change their behaviors to create a more productive workplace."[188] Research has shown that when a leadership assessment is delivered and executed correctly, it can change the behavior and character of the leader

---

[188] Edleson, 58.

in positive ways improving their leadership capabilities in those they lead and in the workplace.

The following tables below will aid a leader in conducting a 360 servant leadership assessment within their organization, identifying key areas of proficiency and those that require strengthening and growth.

Table 1
Twenty-One 360 Survey Questions

Number	Question	Group	Result
1.	I am open to sharing my personal problems with others for guidance and direction.	Personal Sensitivity	
2.	I care about the well-being of all those interact with.	Personal Sensitivity	
3.	I show care and compassion to others when they are emotionally down and low in spirit.	Personal Sensitivity	
4.	I often give back to the broader group or public for group success.	Developing Group Significance	
5.	I volunteer for group events where I can make a difference in others' lives.	Developing Group Significance	
6.	I volunteer for group events where I can make a difference in others' lives.	Developing Group Significance	
7.	I can sense when something is not right or out of alignment of normal work routines.	Environmental Awareness	

8.	When faced with a complex problem, I can think through it logically and effectively.	Environmental Awareness	
9.	I am able to integrate new innovative and creative thoughts/ideas and concepts in the workplace.	Environmental Awareness	
10.	I have the flexibility to take risks.	Inspirational Motivation	
11.	I can make important decisions without supervisor/ manager approval.	Inspirational Motivation	
12.	I often consult others before making an important decision.	Inspirational Motivation	
13.	Helping others with their career growth and development is a priority for me.	Encouraging others to Grow and Achieve Success	
14.	I help others attain career goals and achievements.	Encouraging others to Grow and Achieve Success	
15.	I am willing to invest personal time to help others grow and succeed.	Encouraging others to Grow and Achieve Success	
16.	I put others career goals above mine.	Elevating Others Above Myself	
17.	I am willing to sacrifice personal time and gain for others success and achievement.	Elevating Others Above Myself	

18.	I make the effort to improve others work environments and reduce their workload.	Elevating Others Above Myself	
19.	I have high ethical standards for myself and those I interact with.	Ethical Conduct	
20.	I am authentic and honest in my interactions with everyone.	Ethical Conduct	
21.	I put honest ethical behavior and standards above financial success and career gain for myself and others.	Ethical Conduct	

Table 2
Group Definitions

Number	Group
1.	*Personal sensitivity.* A focus on the concern for others well-being and thier state of mind.
2.	*Developing group significance.* A desire for success of the group above one's own success and achievement.
3.	*Environmental awareness.* Having the knowledge and skillsets to help others achieve success.
4.	*Inspirational motivation.* Supporting and motivating others during complex problems, guiding them through the process to achieve a solution or positive outcome.
5.	*Encouraging others to grow and achieve success.* Coaching, mentoring, supporting, and facilitating development and growth activities for others' success and gain.
6.	*Elevating others above myself.* Living and displaying servant leadership characteristics that other's work success is a priority above oneself.

7.	*Ethical conduct.* Treating others with the utmost respect in honest and authentic leadership behaviors without sacrificing leadership character values for financial gain or career promotion achievement.

Each participant was asked to score each question based upon the following response with associated rating (Table 3):

Table 3
Survey Rating

Score:	Response:	Rating:
5	= Highly Agree	100%
4	= Agree	80%
3	= Neutral (neither agree nor disagree)	60%
2	= Disagree	40%
1	= Highly Disagree	20%

Once the twenty-one questions have been scored based on the scoring, the results can be synthesized to generate a final report. From there, charts and graphs can be developed to aid in building a narrative of those areas where the leader is strong and those needing strengthening. A formalized report can then be produced for the leader to understand what the results are indicating for next steps.

This study demonstrates that servant leadership is unique in that it extends beyond prior leadership theories of transformational, leader-member exchange, transactional, and other noted theories because of the natural desire of the leader to serve followers first. While other leadership theories drive follower behaviors to achieve individual leader self-interest or organizational goals achievement as a number one priority, servant leadership's primary focus is the follower's success, including their well-being, and the improvement of all people in society.

CHAPTER 10

Integrating and Applying Servant Leadership in Workplace Leadership Programs

Today's modern leadership programs have a variety of approaches, methods, tools, and processes at their disposal to improve leadership capabilities. Traditionally, when a new system or methodology is introduced to an organization, training or readiness is provided to immerse or incorporate the new concept into the organization's culture and daily workstreams. While introducing a new approach may change the organization, new techniques lose traction and stick ability. Employees typically fall back into their prior ways of completing their work instead of fully adopting the new process. How can leaders, especially servant leaders, ensure stick ability of new methods and approaches for improved individual and organizational performance, with a desire to become an integral part of their culture?

The purpose of this section is to provide change leaders and their organizations a practical method of ensuring new knowledge, training, learnings, or leadership approaches are integrated and applied throughout the culture of the organization, starting with leadership and then flowing down to its followers. Several servant leadership models have already been discussed in chapter one. This practical application discussion will build upon servant leadership characteristics discussed earlier. The primary focus will be on servant leadership application in today's workplace leadership development programs.

148

Execution Plan (30, 60, 90 Days)

This section will discuss a thirty, sixty, and ninety-day implementation plan for leaders to apply in their organizations. This first part focuses on the servant leader implementing the program to work closely with the team leads and people managers who have direct reports. In large organizations, it is nearly impossible for a leader executing this plan to work directly with each individual due to scalability limitations. However, suppose the leader who implements this plan develops their direct reports as servant leaders? In that case, they will, in turn, build and grow their followers as servant leaders, having a multiplier outcome of servant leaders. The critical virtue here is empowerment of the leader who will ultimately practice and apply servant leadership characteristics with their followers. Empowering provides followers complete control for decision-making and increasing authority. To empower followers, a servant leader must "model the way, inspire a shared vision, challenge the process, enable others to act, and encourage the heart."[189]

In the first month, at the beginning of the thirty-day mark, the leader delivers 360 Servant Leadership Assessment from chapter 9. 360 Degree Feedback Assessments have been conducted in organizations over the last twenty years to evaluate a leader or individual's strengths and areas for growth/improvement. "These employee assessments collect data from colleagues, subordinates, and clients—hence the name 360 degree appraisal—to help illuminate how well employees are performing and how individuals might need to change their behaviors to create a more productive workplace."[190] Research has shown that when an assessment is delivered and executed correctly, it can change the leader's behavior and character positively, improving their leadership capabilities in those they lead and the workplace overall. The leader who executes this plan will also deliver servant leadership and modern-day application presentations to the

---

[189] Kouzes and Posner, 15.
[190] Edleson, 58.

teams whom the leaders report to. This form of engagement will strengthen concepts from both approaches to leadership development and growth.

In the second month, at the beginning of the sixty-day mark, the leader implementing this program will compile the assessment results, analyze the data, and conduct formal reviews with each assessment participant, highlighting strengths and areas for growth improvement. This will include recommendations to strengthen their servant leadership approach and daily practices. Next, this will encourage and motivate leaders to apply and purposely practice Servant Leadership in and outside of their daily work rhythm through empowerment. The result will be a multiplier effect of their key learnings and approach to those the leader they come in daily contact.

In the third month, at the beginning of the ninety-day mark, continue to deliver assessments and offer those in nonpeople manager roles to strengthen their knowledge and application of the leadership content provided from both approaches in table 1 below.

Table 1
30-, 60-, 90-Day Plan

30 Days	60 Days	90 Days
1. Conduct 360 Servant Leadership Assessments to team leads and people managers. 2. Deliver Servant Leadership and Modern-Day Application Presentation to all teams.	1. Analyze and deliver Leadership Assessment reports, findings, and results to all participants.	1. Continue to deliver assessment to followers in organization.

Developing and Strengthening
Positive Leadership Behaviors

While the plan articulated above focuses on implementing and executing the thirty-, sixty-, ninety-day plan, another approach can also be applied. This section will discuss the feedforward approach,[191] in which the leader purposefully acknowledges a character trait or behavior they wish to change or strengthen. The second approach involves the individual (people manager or individual contributor) purposely applying servant leadership characteristics within and outside their organization.

Feedforward Approach

The traditional method to improving leaders and followers from various feedback approaches has continued to be a common approach to improving performance and developing people. Followers need feedback on what to change or improve, and leaders in tandem also need similar feedback for themselves. However, the challenge with feedback is that it has already occurred and likely irrelevant for future development and improvement for leaders and followers. M. Goldsmith, author of article, "Try Feedforward instead of Feedback," further states, feedback "focuses on the past, on what has already occurred—not on the infinite variety of things that can be in the future. As such feedback can be limited and static, as opposed to expansive and dynamic."[192] To implement a feedforward approach, a leader must acknowledge a behavior characteristic they would like to change or strengthen. And then, in tandem with an accountability partner, monitor their behavior for the characteristic, or desired behavior identified, reporting back to the leader over specific period results of change with suggestions and recommendations. This approach has become a more preferred method for leadership

---

[191] (Goldsmith 2003).
[192] Goldsmith, 38.

development resulting in increased leader enthusiasm, innovation, and change to become a dynamic and effective leader. Table 2 below is a sample table a leader and accountability partner would employ, integrating servant leadership characteristics. Further details for feed-forward implementation can be found in the article by Goldsmith.

Table 2

Application Chart

Servant Leadership Characteristics/ Behaviors	Acknowledgment	Accountability Partner	Time Period/ Interval	Check Point Frequencies	Confirmed Change
Listening					
Empathy					
Healing					
Awareness					
Persuasion					
Conceptualization					
Foresight					
Stewardship					
Growth					
Community Building					

Individual Application

As highlighted in table 3, a second approach is the individual applying servant leadership characteristics in daily routines and responsibilities. This applies to both the leader and follower. Alternatively, Patterson (2003) highlights seven virtuous constructs of servant leadership below as discussed earlier in chapter 1. Here the leader would choose a virtue every day and purposely apply it during throughout their workday. It makes no difference in or outside of their organization. The goal is to begin using and practice daily, acknowledging application. The figure below can be modified per the leader's desire to delve deeper into the implementation of their lives.

Table 3

Individual Application in the Workplace

Virtue	Application/Best Practice	Completed: (Yes or No)
Agapao Love	• Acknowledge other people outside your inner circle. • Engage in self-less acts to another person or group who is in an unfortunate circumstance, situation.	
Humility	• Positively encouraging and praising someone else for their efforts above yours.	
Altruism	• Do something special without others knowing or seeing. Give or donate something of value to you for others to appreciate – money, time, resources.	
Vision	• Invest in someone's future by encouraging and providing opportunities for them to grow and excel. • Provide a path to success and encourage and challenge them to achieve it.	
Trust	• Delegate Sr. leadership responsibilities to grow follower competencies and strengths.	
Empowerment	• Give someone full autonomy for an important task or project and let them know they are leading with little oversight or guidance from leadership. • Assume the risk and if they fail, constructively review for future improvement.	
Service	• Invest your people by asking what you can do to better serve them in their role. • Genuinely show care, compassion, humility, empathy, and concern for their well-being.	

Measuring Success and Expected Outcomes

While training, knowledge transfer, and practical application have been offered, how will leaders and their organizations know this leadership development approach will be successful? What are the change signals, and what evidence of change will be present for all to see and appreciate? Are we seeing a positive difference in the organization, and is this reflected in all the listening systems? Are followers achieving a state of being or self-actualization in living out the dare to lead and servant leadership characteristics or virtues? According to Greenleaf in his seminal writing, "The Servant as Leader:"

> The Servant-Leader is servant first... It begins with the natural feeling that one wants to serve, to serve first. The conscious choice begins to aspire to lead... The best test and difficult to administer is this: Do those served grow in

persons? Do they, while being served, become healthier, wiser, freer, more autonomous, and more likely themselves to become servants? And, what is the effect on the least privileged in society? Will they benefit, or at least not further be harmed?[193]

Servant leadership is considered successful when followers in the organization grow and achieve a state of being or self-actualization. Several methods and listening systems can be employed, such as occupational health surveys, town halls, in-person meetings to capture organization and leader feedback for improvement. However, actual leadership development begins when there is a change in heart, resulting in character maturity and individual growth.

---

[193] Greenleaf, 7.

CONCLUSION/FINAL THOUGHTS

So after reading this book, are you confident that you can now lead more effectively as a servant leader? Or if you have already been leading for several years, what areas do you feel need attention to either strengthen or change? Overall, as clearly stated with several examples, love and the love of people is the primary ingredient to the secret sauce of servant leadership. First Corinthians 13:1–3 (NIV), sums this all up:

> If I speak in the tongues of men or of angels, but do not have love, I am only a resounding gong or a clanging cymbal. If I have the gift of prophecy and can fathom all mysteries and all knowledge, and if I have a faith that can move mountains, but do not have love, I am nothing. If I give all I possess to the poor and give over my body to hardship that I may boast, but do not have love, I gain nothing.

BIBLIOGRAPHY

Ackermann, Fran, and Colin Eden. *Making Strategy: Mapping Out Strategic Success.* London: Sage, 2011.

Agosto, Efrain. *Servant Leadership: Jesus and Paul.* Danvers: Chalice Press, 2005.

Altucher, J. *Trade Like Warren Buffett.* 1. Aufl.;1st; ed.: Wiley, 2005.

Anderson, Jon Aarum. "When a Servant Leader Comes a Knocking." *Leadership & Organization Development Journal* 30 (1): 4–15. 2009.

Baldoni, John. *The Leadership Lessons of Dolly Parton.* March 25, 2008.

Barbuto, John E., and Daniel W. Wheeler. "Scale Development and Construct Clarification of Servant Leadership." *Grou & Organizational Management* 31 (3): 300–326. 2006.

Barton, Dominic. "Character: A muscle leaders must develop." *Organizational Dynamics* 1–7. 2019.

Bell, Skip. *Servants and Friends.* Berrien Springs: Andrews University Press, 2014.

Ben-Hur, S., and K. Jonsen. "Ethical leadership: Lessons from moses." *The Journal of Management Development* 31 (9): 962–973. 2012. doi:10.1108/02621711211259901.

Blanchard, Ken, and Renee Broadwell. *Servant Leadership in Action: How You Can Achieve Great Relationships and Results.* Berrett-Koehler Publishers, 2018.

Borcarnea, Mihai C., Joshua Henson, Russell L. Huizing, Michael Mahan, and Bruce E. Winston. *Evaluating Employee Performance through Christian Virtues.* Gewerbestrasse: Springer Publishing AG, 2018.

Brand, A. "Knowledge management and innovation at 3M. Journal of Knowledge Management." *Journal of Knowledge Management* 2 (1): 17–22. 1998.

Britannica, T. Editors of Encyclopaedia. "Book of Judges. Encyclopedia Britannica." 2002. https://www.britannica.com/topic/Book-of-Judges.

Buffett, Warren. *Warren Buffett on Leadership and Trust.* May 11, 2020. https://www.bing.com/videos/search?q=warren+buffett+and+trust&docid=6080528310025978305&mid=C1C873040A-C8A8D6ECC4C1C873040AC8A8D6ECC4&view=detail&-FORM=VIRE.

Burns, J. M. *Leadership.* New York: Harper & Row Publishers, 1978.

Burton, Richard M., Borge Obel, and Dorthe Dojbak Hakonsson. *Organizational Design a Step-by-Step Approach.* Cambridge: Cambridge University Press, 2006.

Cameron, Kim S., and Robert E. Quinn. *Diagnosing and Changing Organizational Culture.* San Francisco: Josey-Bass, 2011.

"Captain Chesley "Sully" Sullenberger retires from US airways." *Airline Industry Information* 1. 2010.

Carbery, Ronan, and Christine Cross. *Human Resource Development A Concise Introduction.* New York: Palmgrave MacMillan Publishing, 2015.

Carleton, Putnam. *Theodore Roosevelt (biography).* New York: William Morrow, 1958.

Castiglione, D. "Accountability. Encyclopedia Britannica." *Encyclopedia Britannica.* 2012. www.britannica.com/topic/accountability.

Colleran, E. "Meowslow's hierachy of needs." *Vetted* 112 (11): 8–9. 2017.

Conger, Jay A. "Charismatic and Transformational leadership in Organizations: an insider's perspective on these developing streams of research." *Leadership Quarterly* 10 (2): 145–179. 1999.

Cooper, M. "The transformational leadership of the apostle paul: A contextual and biblical leadership for contemporary ministry." *Christian Education Journal* 2 (1): 48–61. 2005. doi:10.1177/073989130500200103.

Covey, S. R. *The seven habits of highly effective people: Restoring the character ethic.* New York: Simon and Schuster, 1989.

Crowther, Steven. *Biblical Servant Leadership: An Exploration of Leadership for the Contemporary Context.* Cham: Palgrave Macmillan, 2018.

Cunningham, Lawrence. *Opinion: Trust is the secret sauce that Warren Buffett and others value highly in companies.* December 19, 2020. https://www.marketwatch.com/story/trust-is-the-secret-sauce-in-companies-that-warren-buffett-and-others-value-highly-2020-12-17.

Danker, William. *A Greek-English Lexicon of the New Testament and Other Early Christian Literature: Revised and Edited by Fredrick William Danker 3rd. ed.* Chicago: University of Chicago, 2000.

Deterding, Mark. *Leading Jesus' Way.* Lambertville: Weaving Influence, 2016.

Dierendonck, Dirk van, and Kathleen Patterson. *Servant Leadership: Developments of Theory and Research.* New York: Palmgrave Macmillian, 2010.

Dik, Bryan J., and Ryan D. Duffy. "Calling and Vocation at Work: Defnitions and Prospects for Research and Practice." *The Counseling Psychologist* 37 (3): 424–450. 2009.

D'Souza, J., and M. Gurin. "The universal significance of maslow's concept of self-actualization." *The Humanistic Psychologist* 44 (2): 210–214. 2016.

Duckworth, Angela. *Grit: the power of passion and perseverance | Angela Lee Duckworth.* May 9, 2013. https://www.youtube.com/watch?v=H14bBuluwB8.

Edleson, H. "Do 360 Evaluations Work." *American Psychological Assocation* 43 (10): 58. 2012.

Engstrom, Ted W. *The Making of a Christian Leader.* Grand Rapids: Zondervan, 1976.

Ferch, Shann Ray, Larry C. Spears, Mary McFarland, and Michael R. Carey. *Conversations on Servant-Leadership Insights on Human Courage in Life and Work.* Albany: State University of New York Press, 2015.

Gellerman, Bill, and Ken Hultman. *Balancing Individual and Organizational Values*. San Francisco: Jossey-Bass/Pfeiffer, 2002.

Goldberg, A., and B. Ritter. "Costco CEO Finds Pro-Worker Means Profitability." 2006.

Goldsmith, M. "Try feedforward instead of feedback." *The Journal for Quality and Participation* 26 (3): 38–40. 2003. http://eres.regent.edu:2048/login?url=https://search-proquest-com.ezproxy.regent.edu/docview/219134535?accountid=13479.

n.d. *Great American Business Leaders of The 20th Century*. https://www.hbs.edu/leadership/20th-century-leaders/Pages/details.aspx?profile=james_d_sinegal.

Greenleaf, Robert K. *The Servant as Leader*. Westfield, IN: The Greenleaf Center for Servant Leadership, 1991.

Greenleaf, Robert. *Servant Leadership: A Journey into the Nature of Legitimate Power & Greatness*. New York: Paulist Press, 1991.

———. *Servant Leadership: A Journey into the Nature of Legititmate Power & Greatness*. New York: Paulist Press, 1977.

Gurgaon. "Satya Nadella's First Email To Employees—Why am I here?" *Dataquest*. 2014.

Hertzburg, B. "Deborah and Moses." *Journal for the Study of the Old Testament* 38 (1): 15–33. 2013. doi:10.1177/0309089213492816.

Hines, Gary. "Strategic Foresight." *The Futurist*, 18–21. 2006.

Hoehner, In Elwell, W. A. *Love. Evangelical Dictionary of Theology*. Grand Rapids: Baker Book House Company, 2001.

Hofstede, Geert, Gert Jan Hofstede, and Michael Minkov. *Cultures and Organizations*. New York: McGraw-Hill Publishing, 2010.

Hopping, Clare. "Microsoft's Satya Nadella Reveals New Company Vision." *IT Pro*. 2015.

Hughes, Richard L., Katherine Colarelli Beatty, and David L. Dinwoodie. *Becoming A Strategic Leader*. San Franciso: Jossey-Bass, 2014.

Johnson, Craig E., and Michael Z. Hackman. *Leadership A Communication Perspective Seventh Edition*. Long Grove: Waveland Press, 2018.

Joseph, E. Errol, and Bruce E. Winston. "A Correlation of Servant Leadership, Leader Trust, and Organizational Trust." *Leadership & Organizational Development Journal* 26 (1): 6–22. 2003.

Koulopoulos, Thomas. "What I Learned About Leadership Working For Ross Perot." *Inc. Magazine.* July 10, 2019. https://www.inc.com/thomas-koulopoulos/what-i-learned-about-leadership-working-for-ross-perot.html.

Kouzes, James M., and Barry Z. Posner. *The Leadership Challenge.* San Francisco: The Leadership Challenge A Wiley Brand, 2012.

Kudonoo, Schroeder, and Boysen-Rotelli. "An Olympic Transformation: Creating an Organizational Culture that Promotes Healthy Conflict." *Organizational Development Journal* 30 (2): 52–56. 2012.

Lodice, Emilio F. "The Courage to Lead: The Leadership Legacies of." *The Journal of Values-Based Leadership* 10 (1): 1–24. 2017.

Maclariello, J. "Lessons in leadership and management from nehemiah." *Theology Today (Ephrata, PA.),* 60 (3): 397–407. 2003. doi:10.1177/004057360306000309.

Mandela, N. R. *Long Walk to Freedom. The Autobiography of Nelson Mandela.* New York: Hachette Book Group, 1994.

"Mandela's legacy inspires workers to renew commitment to justice and equality for all: OFL statement for december 10, 2013 international human rights day "vision without action is just a dream, action without vision just passes the time, vision with actio." *Marketwired.* 2013. http://eres.regent.edu/login?url=https://www-proquest-com.ezproxy.regent.edu/trade-journals/mandelas-legacy-inspires-workers-renew-commitment/docview/1466161984/se-2?accountid=13479.

McGregor, J. "CEO satya nadella's love of literary quotes: In a memo to employees that lays out his vision for the company, satya nadella again takes a page from his favorite books." *Washington: WP Company LLC d/b/a The Washington Post,* 2014.

McNulty, E. J. "Leading Through COVID-19." *MIT Sloan Blogs,* 2020.

Miller. "Transforming Leadership: What Does Love Have To Do With It?" *Transformation* 23 (2): 94–106. 2006.

Morris, J. M. *The origins of UNICEF, 1946-1953*. Lexington Books, 2015.

Nadella, S., and J. Euchner. "Navigating digital transformation: An Interview with Satya Nadella." *Research Technology Management* 61 (4): 11–15. 2018. doi:10.1080/08956308.2018.1471272.

Nadella, Satya. *Hit Refresh: Our Quest to Rediscover Microsoft's Soul and Imagine a Better Future for Everyone*. New York: Harper Collins, 2017.

Northouse, Peter G. *Leadership Theory and Practice*. New Delhi: Sage Publications, 2013.

Novak, Michael. *Business As A Calling*. New York: The Free Press, 1996.

Ohonme, Manny. *Sole Purpose: Shoes of Hope From the Feet of a Samaritan*. Charlotte: LifeBridge Books, 2009.

Olesen, T. "Global Political Iconography: The Making of Nelson Mandela." *American Journal of Cultural Sociology* 3 (1): 34–64. 2015. doi:10.1057/ajcs.2014.14.

Oppenheim, C. E. "Nelson Mandela and the Power of Ubuntu." *(Basel, Switzerland)* 3 (2): 369–388. 2012.

Papia, Fahmina Ahmed. *Leadership Qualities—Style, Traits, and Skills of James Sinegal*. 2021. https://www.thestrategywatch.com/leadership-qualities-style-traits-skills-james-sinegal/#:~:text=Leadership%20Style%20of%20James%20Sinegal%20If%20you%20observe,operations%2C%20he%20prioritized%20the%20well-being%20of%20the%20business.

Patterson, Kathleen. "Servant Leadership: A theoretical Model." *Servant Leadership Research Roundtable* 1–10. 2003.

Patterson, Kathleen. "Servant Leadership: A theoretical Model." *Servant Leadership Research Roundtable* 1–10. 2003. https://www.regent.edu/wp-content/uploads/2020/12/patterson_servant_leadership.pdf.

Perot, R. "Change is Fun." *Executive Excellence* 13 (9): 10. Perot, R. (1996). Change is fun. Executive Excellence, 13(9), 10. 1996. Retrieved from http://eres.regent.edu/login?url=https://www-proquest-com.ezproxy.regent.edu/trade-journals/change-is-fun/docview/204541075/se-2?accountid=13479.

Rainey, J. "An upbeat view of a cold new york day: Chesley Sullenberger and tom hanks laud the 'common humanity' of Clint Eastwood's film 'Sully'." *Variety* 333 (8): 1–3. 2016.

Reeves, M., and J. Fuller. "When SMART goals are not so smart." *MIT Sloan Manageement Review* 59 (4): 1–5. 2018.

Rekdal, Andreas. "Mission Matters: how Blackbaud Build A Culture arond Passion for Nonprofits." *Insider Spotlight,* 2018.

Robert, Greenleaf. *The Servant as Leader.* Newton Centre: The Robert K. Greenleaf Center, 1970.

Rokeach, M. *The Nature of Human Values.* New York: The Free Press, 1973.

Schein, Edgar H. *Organizational Culture and Leadership 4th Ed.* San Francisco: Jossey-Bass, 2010.

Schein, Edgar H., and Peter Schein. *Organizatonal Culture and Leadership 5th Ed.* Hoboken: John Wiley & Sons, 2017.

Seijts, Gerard, and Kimberly Young Milani. "The myriad ways in which COVID-19." *Organizational Dynamics* 8, 2019.

Sendjaya, Sen. *Personal and Organizational Excellence through Servant Leadership: Learning to Serve.* Switzerland: Springer International, 2015.

Sinek, Simon. "Build your Life with your Values | Simon Sinek | Ted 2015." 2015.

"South Africa's new era (transcript of Mandela's speech at Cape Town city hall, 'Africa It Is Ours!')." *New York Times,* 1990. https://www.nytimes.com/1990/02/12/world/south-africa-s-new-era-transcript-mandela-s-speech-cape-town-city-hall-africa-it.html?pagewanted=all&src=pm.

Spears, Larry C. *Insights on Leadership: Service, Stewardship, Spirit, and Servant-Leadership.* New York: John Wiley and Sons, 1998.

Steger, Michael F., N. K. Pickering, J. Y. Shin, and B. J. Dik. "Calling in Work: Secular or Sacred?" *Jouran of Career Assessment* 18 (1): 82–86. 2010.

Stilwell, Blake. *Why Ross Perot Was A Veteran To Be Admired.* April 29, 2020. https://www.wearethemighty.com/mighty-trending/ross-perot-veteran/.

Stone, L. "Ross Perot." *In Gale Literature: Contemporary Authors,* 2019. https://link.gale.com/apps/doc/H1000114536/LitRC?u=vic_ regent&sid=summon&xid=79cc9692.

Sweeney, Marvin A. *The Pentateuch.* Nashville: Abingdon Press, 2017.

Teague, J. "Dolly parton's tough upbringing gave her core values." *Express Online,* 2015.

Winston, B. *Be a leader for God's Sake: from values to behaviors.* Virginia Beach: Regent University, School of Leadership Studies, 2002.

Winston, Bruce. "Extending Patterson's Servant Leadership Model: Explaining How Leaders and Followers Interact in a Circular Model." *Servant Leadership Roundtable* 1–9. August 2003.

Wright, N. T. *After You Believe: Why Christian Character Matters.* New York: Harperone, 2012.

Wright, Thomas A., and Kyle J. Emich. "Character in crisis: The benefits of the 3-H apporach to character development." *Organizational Dynamics* 1–10. 2019.

Zak, Paul J. *The Neuroscience of Trust: Management behaviors that foster employee engagement.* January–February 2017. https://hbr. org/2017/01/the-neuroscience-of-trust.

Zhao, Q., C. Dickson, J. Thornton, P. Solis, and E. A. Wentz. "Articulating strategies to address heat resilience using spatial optimization and temporal analysis of utility assistance data of the salvation army metro phoenix." *Applied Geography (Sevenoaks)* 122 (102241): 1–10. 2020.

ABOUT THE AUTHOR

Dr. Peter K. Scheuermann Sr. has over thirty-five years' experience in technical consulting, training, organizational development, coaching, and strategic advisement from small businesses to Fortune 500 clients. However, his inner passion and desire lies in helping others achieve character development and fulfillment in their lives, evangelizing thought leadership in organizations. Dr. Scheuermann currently works for Microsoft as Modern Work Architect within the Office 365 Engineering Group and serves principal managing partner for The Scheuermann Leadership and Consulting Group. He is also a graduate of Regent University's Doctor of Strategic Leadership (DSL) program with a concentration in servant leadership. He can be contacted at https://www.linkedin.com/in/peterkscheuermann/.